FOUR SPIRITUAL CRISES
IN MID-CENTURY
AMERICAN FICTION

FOUR SPIRITUAL CRISES IN MID-CENTURY AMERICAN FICTION

by Robert Detweiler

University of Florida Monographs

HUMANITIES

No. 14, Fall 1963

LIBRARY
BRYAN COLLEGE
DAYTON, TENN. 37321

Essay Index Reprint Series

Originally Published by
UNIVERSITY OF FLORIDA PRESS

BOOKS FOR LIBRARIES PRESS
FREEPORT, NEW YORK

58829

Copyright © 1964 by The Board of Commissioners of
State Institutions of Florida

Reprinted 1970 by arrangement with Robert Detweiler

INTERNATIONAL STANDARD BOOK NUMBER:

0-8369-1799-5

LIBRARY OF CONGRESS CATALOG CARD NUMBER:

78-121461

PRINTED IN THE UNITED STATES OF AMERICA

ACKNOWLEDGMENTS

The present work was written as part of a project made possible by a twelve-month postdoctoral grant from the University of Florida Graduate School; it is a pleasure to acknowledge that generous aid. I am indebted further to Professor T. Walter Herbert for guidance in shaping the study to monograph form, as well as to Professors Harry R. Warfel and Richard H. Hiers, who read the manuscript and offered helpful criticisms. Finally, I wish to acknowledge the influence of my brother, the Reverend Richard C. Detweiler, in conversations with whom the original idea of the study was conceived.

ROBERT DETWEILER

CONTENTS

1. RELIGION IN POSTWAR AMERICAN FICTION

In spite of the secular temper of our "post-Christian era," American fiction of at least the last decade and a half has reflected an increasing interest in religion. Christ figures, Old and New Testament imagery, metaphors of spiritual doubt and affirmation have been offered in scores of novels and short stories.. Within a still more recent period, for the most part within the past five years, certain authors have contributed to a religious-literary liaison that moves far beyond the stage of symbolic indirection. They have resurrected the individual religious experience to serve as the motif, fundamental situation, or point of conflict in their stories. It may be incorrect to label the new interest even as a resurrection, because serious fiction in America has never been concerned with the inner workings of religion. The popular religious novel, of course, has exploited that domain since the 1840's. The life-of-Christ historical romance, the conversion story, the what-would-Jesus-do fiction of the social gospel movement have all focused upon religious transformations. The books of Charles Sheldon, Grace Livingston Hill, Lloyd Douglas, and Frank Slaughter populate many a Sunday School library and decorate many a middle-class Protestant home unreceptive to, say, Twain, Melville, James, or Faulkner. Yet the religious writers, their tremendous appeal and economic success notwithstanding, have seldom met the standards of literary criticism and have not, therefore, influenced the mainstream of American fiction.

America's better novelists have either treated religion only as a part of the general cultural setting or have ignored it altogether. Hawthorne, through his guilt-obsessed clergy, and Melville, through his tormented *isolatos,* dramatized the conflict of the Calvinist conscience without ever limiting themselves to the alternatives of grace or damnation. The naturalists Crane, Norris, and Dreiser implied at best a natural morality divorced from theological considerations. Later in the twentieth century, Sherwood Anderson, Sinclair Lewis, and Nathanael West, far from providing sympathetic treatment, turned the popular image of organized Protestantism to ridicule. American novels with a sympathetic treatment of religious persons and ideas have appeared, of course, such as Willa Cather's *Death Comes for the Archbishop* and Faulkner's *Requiem for a Nun*, but they are the exception rather than the rule.

The post-World-War-II generation, I submit, has produced novelists who are more vitally and directly concerned with religion in fiction than any preceding age. It is not a matter of religiously committed authors lending their talents to church or synagogue to turn out still more inferior propagation-of-the-faith fiction. Neither is it simply an intensifying of the Christian symbolism pervading the works of Steinbeck, Hemingway, and Faulkner, although there is no denying the influence of those older writers upon the younger generation. These talented artists of the 1950's and '60's, with demonstrated ability to compose good fiction, have taken the religious element earnestly and objectively enough to render it an integral part of their creations.

I have chosen four authors to represent the new impulse. They are William Styron, John Updike, Philip Roth, and J. D. Salinger. What they have in common is obvious: they are all Americans; they all still qualify as "young" writers; they have all, while not yet establishing solid reputations, received critical and popular recognition as exceptionally fine artists. In their divergence they stand for varying attitudes in the new fiction which agree, if nowhere else, in the common concern with religion. Styron, first, has had more than casual connections with the South even if he cannot be identified with the newer southern school. His first novel inhabited a Virginia setting (Styron's own background) and his third, although located mainly in Italy, has the American South as its native foundation. Even more significantly, Styron's writing is marked—almost cursed—by the heavy, brooding, chaotic style of the Faulknerian heritage that turns naturally to the old fascination with problems of unwitting depravity, obsessive guilt, and salvation through despair. In this aspect Styron has revealed his kinship with Flannery O'Connor, Madison Jones, and Eudora Welty even though he has stressed neither southern regionalism nor the southern myth.

Updike, in contrast, is among the writers of northern urbanity and clinical sexuality who nonetheless display a feeling for modern Protestantism once comfortably entrenched in small towns and now caught up in the secularism of the expanding northeastern megalopolis. Like John Cheever, like James Baldwin minus the racial bur-

2

den, or like Peter De Vries *sans* satire, he treats the individual who is haunted by the devil of adolescent catechism classes while indulging in the slick, packaged pleasures of industrialized life. The search is for a relief from boredom and, lingering just behind it, a relief from the fear of acknowledging the senselessness of existence that outmoded religious forms cannot assuage.

Roth belongs to the group of sensitive Jewish novelists who have managed to make the plight of the contemporary American Jew a metaphor of the religious sterility of the whole country. Along with Bernard Malamud, Saul Bellow, and Herbert Gold, Roth reflects the struggle to retain the values of orthodoxy while yielding to an essentially antagonistic cultural pattern. His characters fight for a Jewish identity, confused *schlemiels* trying to distinguish their shadows from the shifting light and dark of the Protestant paradox. Plagued by an inbred morality, they have nowhere to anchor it.

Salinger perhaps forms a direction of his own. If so, his is an eclectic perspective that in its breadth and corresponding absence of depth mirrors the status-conscious embrace of our religiosity. Zen wisdom, Roman Catholic piety, and Jewish fraternalism merge, catalyzed by precocious diction, to thwart the bugbear of Protestant conformity, but what results is a supercilious intellectuality that needs the contrasting crudeness of *hoi polloi* to underscore its own enlightened vision. At bottom it is not much of a vision at all, only a virtuosity that dazzles where it cannot heal. Language-play replaces profundity for Salinger; his reliance upon the power of words to exorcise spiritual frustrations is more an inadvertent illustration of the glib Marble Collegiate Christianity, with its faith in positive thought, than an answer to it.

I do not maintain that the new awareness of religion affects all postwar American fiction. The novelists of war, for example, have excluded it. James Jones, Norman Mailer, and Joseph Heller have depicted the soldier's and the flyer's hell of Europe and of the Pacific without the relief of a saving vision.[1] Nor do I claim that the four writers necessarily give evidence of commitment to a particular doctrine. Certainly they do not fit into the category of the vogue that Leslie Fiedler disparagingly called "the hip pieties of the fif-

---

1. An exception would be the Roman Catholic R. O. Bowen's *The Weight of the Cross* (New York: Alfred A. Knopf, 1951), a novel treating the religious conversion of an American soldier in a Japanese prison camp. Incidentally, I make little comment on Catholic fiction as a separate category

3

ties."[2] They distinguish themselves from the Dharma bum mystics of Jack Kerouac and from Henry Miller's orgiastic ecstasies by a surprising theological sophistication. Without serving as flunkies to theology, without revealing the extent of their knowledge of modern theological positions, they have offered compelling views of American man and his religious situation, compelling not only because they are esthetically well-wrought but because they treat through concrete examples what twentieth-century theologians have been discussing in their own discipline and in their own terminology.

The main intent of my study is to demonstrate that a new attitude toward religion in fiction, as I have initially described it, does in fact exist. To that end I will examine a novel apiece by the four authors, in which is dramatized the experience that is the apex of religious striving: the individual spiritual crisis that leads to the acceptance or rejection of God. Without suggesting that their efforts constitute a "crisis fiction" comparable to contemporary crisis theology, I will seek to indicate a common concern for religion as "the dimension of depth," as Paul Tillich calls it, that impels this quartet to consider the modern American dilemma as a personal, spiritual one demanding a personal, spiritual solution. Rather than ignoring or ridiculing religion according to the naturalist tradition, rather than interpreting it as a psychological or sociological phenomenon after the Freudian or Marxist schools, they choose to treat the crisis, its central manifestation, as a valid aspect, perhaps even as the distinctive event, of human existence. Their novels, providing ideal examples of serious religion in serious fiction, invite a combined literary-theological analysis. By interpreting the four crises in the light of familiar theological positions, I hope to show that they indeed possess an overriding religious relevance and that they function as the products of a literary perspective that draws from theology for its ultimate orientation even while it transforms the theological mode of expression.

Such a treatment, of course, raises more questions than it an-

---

because America, unlike England or France, has simply not produced any consistently first-rate Catholic novelists. The good writers who were born Catholic (Fitzgerald, Hemingway, Katherine Anne Porter) left the church; the general quality of Catholic fiction has not surpassed the level of Protestant literary propaganda.

2. Leslie A. Fiedler, *No! in Thunder, Essays in Myth and Literature* (Boston: Beacon Press, 1960), ix. All quotations by permission of the publisher.

swers; in the concluding pages I want to recognize a few of them. What, for example, has happened to the American spirit that it should demand a literary concern with religion? What is it in the American present that provides a sympathetic context for the liaison? And finally, what are some implications of the relationship for the future of American fiction and American theology?

2. WILLIAM STYRON
AND THE COURAGE TO BE

In his widely praised first novel, *Lie Down In Darkness,* William Styron gave initial evidence of a perceptive religious consciousness oriented to the existential position. Now, in *Set This House on Fire,* he has written a novel suggestive of the tenets of existential theology.[1] The information that the book is existential is not new.[2] The point is that there is an existential theology behind the fiction that determines its character and makes the crisis of the protagonist a religious one. Styron has probably read Nietzsche and Sartre; whether he has also read Kierkegaard and Tillich one cannot say; but, at any rate, the vocabulary and the sequence of spiritual events echo Tillich and his Danish predecessor. A comparison between Tillich and Styron should reveal the similarities.

Set This House on Fire is told through a disjointed series of reminiscing conversations and letters. The contorted style, the confusion of first-person narrators, the shifting time sequences, accent the disoriented and chaotic lives of the characters. The story concerns essentially three Americans: Peter Leverett, the observer-narrator; Mason Flagg, the rich and evil sex-obsessed manipulator of persons; and Cass Kinsolving, weak-willed artist, drunkard, and prime object of Flagg's manipulations. The passive framework of the book is set in Virginia, but the action, related in retrospect, takes place mainly in the village of Sambuco, Italy, where Cass is living with his family in expatriate poverty when Leverett arrives as guest of the wealthy Flagg. Cass emerges as the protagonist, since the novel turns on his suffering and journey toward redemption. In Sambuco he has become the tool and plaything of Mason Flagg, receiving his alcohol and keep (for himself and family) as reward for acting the fool for Flagg's amusement. Between Cass and total debasement is only the young Francesca, lovely daughter of a local peasant family, who is

1. Quotations are from *Set This House on Fire,* by William Styron. ©Copyright 1960 by William Styron. Reprinted by permission of Random House, Inc. Page numbers immediately following quotations are from the Signet Books edition (New York: New American Library, 1961).

2. Cf. David L. Stevenson, "Styron and the Fiction of the Fifties," *Critique,* III (Summer, 1960), 47, who speaks of the existential world of Styron and refers (51) to "Cass' Sartre-like explanation" of his crisis.

part servant, part model for Cass, but who is above all the ideal of purity and wholeness for him. When she is mysteriously raped and murdered, Cass blames Flagg for her death and kills him in a horrible moment of mistaken revenge.

Cass' predicament, in spite of its admittedly melodramatic trappings, is ontological. He is obsessed with the mystery of being and the possibility of nothingness, and his dilemma provides a perfect imaginative example of the existential analysis of man's situation as he moves through the (by now) classic pattern: from fundamental anxiety into despair to a final tentative affirmation of being.

Even while adjusting Cass to the existential stance, Styron provides him not only with the religiously introspective and sensitive temperament that Tillich sees characterized in neurotic Western man but also surrounds him with a setting and supporting cast of figures which reflect the supraconfessional concern of Tillich's philosophical theology. It is no accident that the novel is prefaced by a quotation from a sermon of John Donne, who shifted from Roman Catholicism to a sophisticated Anglicanism. Beyond that, Leverett as narrator is careful to describe himself, albeit facetiously, as "white, Protestant, Anglo-Saxon" (8). Cass himself has been an Episcopalian of sorts who sings gospel songs and whose initiatory, most impressive sexual experience was with a passionate Jehovah's Witness; yet he has married Poppy, the devout and simple Catholic. And then there is Luigi, police officer and "Italian Calvinist," as Cass calls him. The significance of these creedal identifications, apart from the fact that Styron and Cass take them seriously, is that they merge to form a distinct religious base for the story while consciously cancelling each other, thus avoiding doctrinal differences that would reduce the ontological concerns of existentialism to dogmatic quibbling. Confronted as he is by the torture of being and nothingness and even drawing his religiosity from the creeds that surround him, Cass implicitly rejects their solutions as too small and finds his answers in the act of living.

Live he does. His wanderings from Virginia over Paris to Italy consist of one long alcoholic and sexual binge that leaves him on the verge of physical and mental breakdown. Yet it is not Cass' appetites that are his real trouble; they constitute only the syndrome of the trouble, which is anxiety, or what Tillich has called the problem of man's finitude. Cass, like Tillich's Western man, has experienced "the threat of nonbeing" and the resultant "paralysis

7

of the will" indicative of separation from God. In traditional terms, he experiences the sinfulness of his being; in Tillich's terms, that sin is the sense of estrangement from being-itself, or God. The resultant anxiety expresses itself psychopathically, socially, sexually, and esthetically. Cass confesses to Leverett that the mess of his life is not the fault of Mason Flagg, his rich and evil angel, but his own fault and the direct result of his frustrated longing for a belief in divinity or at least for a meaning to life. Luigi, the metaphysically minded policeman, articulates the trouble for Cass in numerous conversations. Once he asks,

Do you not sometimes wake up from a long sleep and for those few moments before you are completely awake feel the terror and the mystery of existence? It lasts but for a few seconds but it is the only time when one moves close to eternity. And do you know something? I do not believe in God. Yet for me the awful part is that in a twinkling I am fully awake, and I do not know whether it was that in that movement toward eternity I have come closer to God— or nothingness (316).

That is precisely the agony of Cass' situation. He answers, "I often feel very lonely too, . . . Very lonely. Very terrified." "Then you understand what I mean?" inquires Luigi. "Yes," replies Cass (317). What Cass and Luigi have experienced is not wholly Styron's creation but an established psychological-theological phenomenon. Tillich comments on it thus:

It is impossible for a finite being to stand naked anxiety for more than a flash of time. People who have experienced these moments, as for example some mystics in their visions of the "night of the soul," or Luther under the despair of the demonic assaults, or Nietzsche-Zarathustra in the experience of the "great disgust," have told of the unimaginable horror of it. . . . The basic anxiety, the anxiety of a finite being about the threat of nonbeing, cannot be eliminated. It belongs to existence itself.[3]

That sharp consciousness of infinity coupled with the realization of his own finitude leads Cass into the second stage. The sobering fact that he must someday die leads him to search for a meaning in finite existence that he cannot find.[4] He becomes involved in

3. Paul Tillich, *The Courage to Be* (New Haven and London: Yale Paperbound, Yale University Press, 1959), p. 39.
4. "Anxiety . . . is not the realization of a universal transitoriness, not

senseless suffering; he is filled with despair, Kierkegaard's "sickness unto death," and all attempts to recover himself only involve him deeper. He feels "the anguish and mystery of *myself*" (379), lives in fear of "the bleeding abyss"(386).[5] He ignores his wife and four children, prostitutes his artistic talent by cartooning for a living, and then, as if to confirm his depravity, paints a picture on commission for Flagg (in three days of drunken activity) that is an excellent execution of sheerest phornography. Once more it is Luigi who both describes the situation to Cass and warns him against what he is doing:

Have you not pictured to yourself the whole horrible vista of eternity? . . . The absolute blankness, *il niente, la nullità*, stretching out for ever and ever, the pit of darkness which you are hurling yourself into, the nothingness, the void, the oblivion? (190).

And later Luigi says, in curiously Kafkaesque idiom, "We are serving our sentences in solitary confinement, unable to speak. All of us. Once we were at least able to talk with our Jailer, but now even He has gone away, leaving us alone with the knowledge of insufferable loss" (473). That statement is reminiscent of the Nietzschean "death of God," but as Cass experiences it, it is according to the existentialist program. It is what Tillich maintains is necessary to the encounter with being: the sense of absolute helplessness and hopelessness, into which chasm God himself will enter to give one the "New Being." Cass undergoes what Donne describes in the sermon which prefaces the novel:

What gnashing is not a comfort, what gnawing of the worme is not a tickling, what torment is not a marriage bed to this damnation, to be secluded eternally, eternally, eternally, from the sight of God? (6).

It is when Cass has reached these depths that the mad sequence of events bringing on his saving crisis takes place. Under the excuse of punishing her for petty thievery, Mason Flagg rapes the virgin Francesca, whose innocent love has been the only steadying, almost the redeeming, influence of Cass' life. The hysterical girl excites the

---

even the experience of the death of others, but the impression of those events on the always latent awareness of our own having to die that produces anxiety. Anxiety is finitude, expressed as one's own finitude" (Tillich, p. 35).

5. Cf. Martin Heidegger's "Abgrund" in his *Introduction to Metaphysics* (New York: Anchor Books, Doubleday & Co., 1961), p. 3.

village idiot, who crushes her skull, and Cass, insane with grief and believing Flagg to be the killer, murders Flagg. Since Flagg's death looks like suicide (only Luigi discovers the truth and covers for Cass), Cass is free from the retribution of the law, but what he has suffered and done threatens to drive him to final disintegration. The crisis takes place at dawn after the day of the murders. Returning home from the police station, Cass sits down in his bedroom beside the sleeping Poppy.

I felt drained of strength and will, past thought of grief, past thought of anything except for that old vast gnawing hunger which began to grow and grow in me like a flower. . . . I knew that I had come to the end of the road and had found there nothing at all. There was nothing. There was a nullity in the universe so great as to encompass and drown the universe itself. The value of a man's life was nothing, and his destiny nothingness. What more proof did I need than that I had traveled halfway across the earth in search of some kind of salvation, and had found it, only to have it shattered in my fingertips? . . . I thought of being. I thought of nothingness. I put my head into my hands, and for a moment the sharp horror of *being* seemed so enormous as to make the horror of nothingness less than nothing by its side (465).

Cass has arrived at the point of utter helplessness which Tillich describes. He feels the three types of anxiety that contribute to the situation of despair: anxiety about fate and death, about meaninglessness, and about guilt and condemnation.[6]

The enormous "horror of being" is analyzed by Tillich as the awareness of being that it cannot affirm itself when confronted by the power of nonbeing. Thus the next step is also predictable: the consideration of suicide, or what according to Tillich is the courage *not* to be, in which "the final form of ontic self-affirmation would be the act of ontic self-negation."[7] Cass does contemplate the step of murdering his family and killing himself: "I sat there, wondering if now at last wasn't the moment to take Poppy and the kids in a single swift hell of blood and butchery, and be done with it all forever" (466). But Cass as existential subject cannot commit suicide, for both the anxiety of guilt and of meaninglessness prevent it. Guilt and condemnation "have an infinite weight and cannot be

6. Cf. Tillich, pp. 40 ff.; also Heidegger, p. 141.
7. Tillich, p. 55.

removed by a finite act of ontic self-negation," while meaningless likewise offers "no ontic exit."[8] It is not surprising, then, that Cass is stopped by the echo of Luigi's words shouted at him an hour earlier in the police station: *"Tu pecchi nell'avere tanto senso di colpa!* You sin in this guilt of yours!" (466).

The dawning of the meaning of those cryptic words is the key to Cass' salvation. Luigi's accusation makes Cass aware at last that to persist in his estrangement from himself and from being is the worst kind of nihilism. In Tillich's terms, to refuse to accept himself because of his unacceptability is already a choice of nonbeing over being. Luigi shows Cass both the true nature of his guilt and the paradox of justification. Cass learns that his essential guilt is not the murder of Flagg or the dissolute life preceding it (those are symptomatic), but his fundamental estrangement, his refusal *to be,* and that the courage to be involves an acceptance of oneself in spite of one's unacceptability. Luigi's role is akin to that of Tillich's "healer." "In the . . . psychoanalytic situation, the patient participates in the healing power of the helper by whom he is accepted although he feels himself unacceptable. The healer, in this relationship, does not stand for himself as an individual but represents the objective power of acceptance and self-affirmation. . . . It must be embodied in a person who can realize guilt, who can judge, and who can accept in spite of judgment."[9] Luigi fills that part dramatically. He knows Cass' crime but will not indict him. Through that act of Luigi's, Cass learns something of the traditional idea of grace and moves toward acceptance of himself. That same morning he reconciles himself with his wife and family and decides to return with them to Virginia.

Styron, of course, does not overplay it. He has Cass deny that he has found grace at all. Recalling the experience for Leverett, Cass says:

Now I suppose I should tell you that through some sort of suffering I had reached grace, and how at that moment I knew it, but this would not be true, because at that moment I didn't really know what I had reached or found.

But what follows—and concludes Cass' narration—is a confession as existential as one could imagine:

8. *Ibid.,* p. 56.
9. *Ibid.,* pp. 165-66.

I can only tell you this: that as for being and nothingness, the one thing I did know was that to choose between them was simply to choose being, not for the sake of being, or even the love of being, much less the desire to be forever—but in the hope of being what I could be for a time. This would be an ecstasy. God knows, it would.

As for the rest, I had come back. And that for a while would do, that would suffice (476-77).

In that simple act of choosing being, Cass has used his freedom to make the existential decision. Like Orestes in Sartre's *The Flies*, Cass emerges on the far side of despair to find hope in self-affirmation. But there is a difference between the existentialism of Sartre and Styron. It is not quite the difference between atheistic and theological existentialism, because Styron does not take Cass the whole way toward faith. On the other hand, he moves a good distance along the road. Sartre denies the existence of a God and the possibility of an idealist metaphysic, so that man must literally create meaning for himself, create his essence through existing. Tillich seems to equate being (actually being-itself) with God,[10] and Styron, despite his reluctance to use traditional terminology (similarly a characteristic of Tillich) hints also in that direction. Note what Tillich says on being-itself and God:

Not arguments but the courage to be reveals the true nature of being-itself. By affirming our being we participate in the self-affirmation of being-itself. There are no valid arguments for the "existence" of God, but there are acts of courage in which we affirm the power of being, whether we know it or not. If we know it, we accept acceptance consciously. If we do not know it, we nevertheless accept it and participate in it. And in our acceptance of that which we do not know the power of being is manifest to us.[11]

There is sufficient evidence to maintain that Cass has accepted acceptance and thereby affirmed being, consciously or not. His longing has been for an encounter with the "unconditional" even though he rejects the traditional form of that encounter. What he encounters may be the God so large, so ultimate that he does not rec-

10. Cf. William L. Rowe, "The Meaning of 'God' in Tillich's Theology," *The Journal of Religion*, XLII (October, 1962), 282-83. Rowe argues that Tillich identifies God with being-itself.
11. Tillich, p. 181.

ognize Him as such. His experience, at any rate, is what Donne describes in the prefatory sermon:

God, who, when he could not get into me, by standing, and knocking . . . hath applied his judgements, and shaked the house, this body, with agues and palsies, and set this house on fire, with fevers and calentures, and frighted the Master of the house, my soule, with horrors, and heavy apprehensions, and so made an entrance into me (5-6).

The difference again is that the God Cass encounters is not the God of theism but Tillich's "God above God." "One can become aware of the God above the God of theism in the anxiety of guilt and condemnation when the traditional symbols that enable men to withstand the anxiety of guilt and condemnation have lost their power. . . . *The courage to be is rooted in the God who appears when God has disappeared in the anxiety of doubt.*"[12] In his crisis, Cass has found the courage to be. The power to accept being is the power of grace itself, although Cass will not call it that. In the courage to be, which is both his existential choice and the gift of grace, Cass has had his crucial religious experience, truly religious because it is grounded not on the formulas of dogma but on his own encounter with the deepest and most encompassing elements of life in which he has found meaning.

12. *Ibid.,* pp. 189-90.

3. JOHN UPDIKE AND THE INDICTMENT OF CULTURE-PROTESTANTISM

Like Styron, John Updike revealed a religious awareness in his first novel, *The Poorhouse Fair*, and in his latest, *The Centaur;* while in "Pigeon Feathers," his prize-winning short story of 1962, the plot itself turns on a boy's religious crisis. At first glance, *Rabbit, Run,* Updike's second novel and the one I will discuss, may seem to be a less "religious" book than the others (*The Poorhouse Fair* even has a Christ figure of sorts in the person of old Hook).[1] But in *Rabbit, Run,* upon closer examination, one finds Updike moving from the occasional religiosity of *The Poorhouse Fair* to a fairly clear theological position from which he can do more exactly what he was attempting in the first book: namely, to criticize the impotence of certain social institutions in their cherished American forms. Updike's approach has much in common with neo-orthodoxy and especially with Reinhold Niebuhr's interpretation of man and his criticism of society. There are, to begin with, certain external parallels. Niebuhr's writing is directed mainly to Protestant culture and is itself distinctly Protestant. Updike's novel represents a solid Protestant milieu; his characterizations and implied criticisms are of the Protestant mentality. More significant are the similar central concerns of Niebuhr and Updike. Niebuhr's emphasis has always been upon the problems of social and individual morality. He has spoken, in the first connection, regarding the demonic nature of social "collectives," and, in the second, concerning the two basic forms of sin: man's denial of freedom and responsibility and, on the other hand, his denial of limitations and the assumption of human independence. Updike, in fictional form, treats exactly the same things: the failure of the social institutions in the small Pennsylvania town and the dual drives of the protagonist toward irresponsibility and independence.

Unlike *Set This House on Fire,* the story of *Rabbit, Run* is easy

1. John Updike, *Rabbit, Run* (New York: Alfred A. Knopf, 1960). All quotations by permission of the publisher. Page numbers immediately following quotations are from the Crest Book reprint (New York: Fawcett World Library, 1962).

14

to retell. Harry "Rabbit" Angstrom, the 26-year-old protagonist, is an ex-high-school basketball hero in the eastern Pennsylvania town of Mt. Judge, caught in the problems of young marriage and parenthood and of an unsatisfying job.[2] The early part of the novel is concerned with Rabbit's escape from Janice, his alcoholic, pregnant, and TV-addicted wife, and from Nelson, his little son. One evening, on impulse, he heads in his car for the South, drawn by a vague vision of sunshine and ease. He gets lost in Maryland and returns home the next morning, not to Janice but to Tothero, his old coach. He meets and moves in with Ruth, a prostitute, and concerns himself the next few weeks with making love to her and parrying the attempts of Eccles, Janice's Episcopalian minister, to get him home. There is a brief period of reconciliation when Janice gives birth to a daughter, and Rabbit goes home for a new start. But after a few days there is another fight and Rabbit leaves once more. Janice turns to alcohol again and in a drunken stupor drowns the baby. Rabbit comes back for the funeral but breaks up the graveyard ceremony by suddenly explaining to the horrified mourners that the death was not his fault but his wife's. He runs away and goes to Ruth, who rejects him when he will not promise to divorce his wife and marry her. At the end of the book, Rabbit is running again in the night, not going anywhere, just running.

One might ask where the crisis appears in the novel, and particularly, to what extent there is a distinctly religious crisis at all. Actually, the whole novel is the record of a crisis that begins when Rabbit first leaves his wife, heightens at the death of his baby daughter, and continues as the book comes to a close. The consistent use of the present tense underscores the immediacy of the crisis; the power of the novel as a whole is mainly in Updike's ability to sustain the tension of crisis; Rabbit's nervous movement throughout serves as a physical metaphor of his inner crisis. The peculiar religious nature of the crisis will become explicit, I think, during the comparison of Rabbit's situation, as example, with the analysis of Niebuhr.

The indictment of what I have called culture-Protestantism appears in *Rabbit, Run* as the first total impression, and it seems to

---

2. Some reviewer or graduate student somewhere must have already commented on the irony of Rabbit's last name: Angstrom—Angst Strom—stream of fear. *Angst* is of course a chic word in existential circles, while *Strom* can hint at Rabbit's incessant running.

be a true one.[3] Rabbit's tragedy is not only that he has no inner resources but that none of the natural and social institutions of his environment are able to help him. Rabbit himself is the epitome of the "nice guy" who with a reasonable amount of support from his community could live a respectable and productive life. Yet it is precisely the failure of the community and the institutions that comprise it which causes Rabbit's own existence to be a failure. Neither marriage, parenthood, vocation, school, nor church can provide him with a good reason for living or with a reason for taking up the responsibilities that each of them offers. As critic J. A. Ward says, "Thus the socially responsible are less alive than Rabbit. They are seen as denying their inner reality for the sake of mass delusions."[4]

Updike presents each institution as a travesty. Rabbit finds a whore who is a better homemaker than his wife. His son is a pawn between the in-laws; and his daughter dies through gross carelessness. His job is first as a barker for the MagiPeel Kitchen Peeler, then as a yardman, then as a used-car salesman. His old high school coach mouths platitudinous tripe about Life ("the will to win," "the sacredness of achievement"). The pastors are either stuck in a myopic conservatism or plagued by their own doubts about the church. But, according to Gordon Harland's interpretation of Niebuhr, "Man has his being in relationships. The truly significant is what happens between man and man."[5] Rabbit's difficulty stems from the fact that he cannot establish relationships, and he cannot because the objects of those relationships have become phony. Ward says that in *Rabbit, Run* one sees "the unconscious mind reacting against all forms of social order."[6] A better way of putting it, I think, would be to state that Rabbit's reaction is against distorted forms of social order. For Niebuhr, says Harland, "The community is both the fulfillment and the frustration of the individual. . . . If he is to enter into true selfhood, the individual must be drawn out of himself into wider relationships. . . . The community sustains his ex-

3. Hardly the same as the formally designated German *Kulturprotestantismus,* but still like it in that Niebuhr also speaks out of a knowledge and condemnation of what it was and in that Updike presents it in its American middle-class ramifications.
4. "John Updike's Fiction," *Critique,* V (Spring-Summer, 1962), 34.
5. *The Thought of Reinhold Niebuhr* (New York: Oxford University Press, 1960), p. 60. All quotations by permission of the publisher.
6. P. 33.

istence and is necessary for self-fulfillment."[7] Rabbit is fighting a losing battle from the start because his community is corrupt, but at least he is still struggling, Updike would have us know, and more consciously than at first appears. "Why else do you like me?" he asks Ruth the prostitute. She answers, " 'Cause you haven't given up. 'Cause in your stupid way you're still fighting."

He loves hearing this; pleasure spins along his nerves, making him feel very tall, and he grins. But the American protest of modesty is instinctive in him, and "The will to achievement" glides out of his mouth mockingly (79).

Rabbit is fighting instinctively what Niebuhr has been fighting since the 1930's. He has been speaking against a false moralism and a belief in human progress that conceals the actual sinful nature of man and society. In 1932 he called his own *Moral Man and Immoral Society* a treatise "directed against the moralists, both religious and secular, who imagine that the egoism of individuals is being progressively checked by the development of rationality or the growth of a religiously inspired goodwill and that nothing but the continuance of this process is necessary to establish social harmony between all the human societies and collectives."[8]

Harland describes the object of Niebuhr's attack as "the prevailing moralism [which] derived its strong crusading social zeal from the heritage of the social gospel. . . . General exhortations to righteousness, peace, love, self-sacrifice, and social concord failing to dip down low enough to encounter any concrete situation or specific evil, often managed to go nicely above the heads of dutiful Sunday listeners and readers of the religious press."[9] In "Christian Moralism in America," Niebuhr wrote, "Our whole difficulty in American Protestantism is in having so long regarded Christianity as synonymous with the simple command to love God and our fellow men, that we have forgotten that the Christian religion is really a great deal more than this."[10] Niebuhr's own approach is to counter the shallow concept of Christian love of God with the concept of *agape,* which is love as the "impossible possibility," the ethical ideal which can never work perfectly in society but which must serve nevertheless as our motive and basis of action in social situations.

7. P. 169.
8. (Rev. ed., New York: Charles Scribner's Sons, 1952), xii. All quotations by permission of the publisher.
9. P. 43.   10. Quoted by Harland, pp. 45-46.

Updike too is concerned with love and especially with the damaging effects of false love relationships. *Rabbit, Run,* in fact, becomes almost a commentary on the false notion of love which excludes the *agape* dimension. Most obvious would be the shallow basis of the relationship Rabbit has with his wife. Since it is mostly physical (their son was born seven months after the marriage) there is little to sustain it when the early novelty wears off, and the situation is underscored by the irony of Rabbit's developing a more "spiritual" bond with his mistress than with his wife. Rabbit's broken connection with his school is illustrated in the inability of the townspeople, who had adulated him as a sports star, to even recognize him any more, and in the exposure of his old coach, who had been his ideal, as a sexual masochist. In his vocation of selling, two of his jobs (as barker and as used-car salesman) depend on his personal appeal, even though both he and his customers know that it is faked ("admitting it's all a fraud but, what the hell, making it likeable" [12]).

Finally, in his relation to the church, Rabbit is met by the forced friendliness of Eccles, Janice's pastor, who "likes" Rabbit partly because he feels he ought to and whose object is to "help" him in some vague ecclesiastical manner. Rabbit's relations to everyone, in fact, are established in terms of whether or not they "like" him: his parents, sister, Coach Tothero, mistress, and Pastor Eccles who do; his in-laws, Tothero's girl, and Lutheran Pastor Kruppenbach who do not. But he never achieves deeper communication, much less communion, with anyone. Even people like Eccles' wife and Janice herself, who are caught in a kind of deeper attraction for him, cannot meet him with any sort of love, nor can Rabbit love. The absence of *agape* in Rabbit's world is the factor which makes that world first a mediocre, then a deadly boring, and finally a demonic place which corrodes and ultimately ruins the sensitive personality.

Niebuhr goes on in *The Nature and Destiny of Man* to amplify his doctrine of love as it relates to individual man in terms of sin and grace (Vol. I, *Human Nature*) and to collective man in terms of evil and justice (Vol. II, *Human Destiny*).[11] Updike's emphasis is of course upon individual man, since he is not writing a political

11. Volume I (New York: Charles Scribner's Sons, 1941); Volume II (New York: Charles Scribner's Sons, 1943). All quotations by permission of the publisher.

18

novel, and here too he parallels Niebuhr's analysis. In this connection Updike, like Niebuhr, treats the cause of human anxiety as the result of the human paradox, the retreat from responsibility into sensuality, and the assertion of the individual's human independence in pride.

According to Niebuhr, man "has always been his own most vexing problem" because of the two conflicting aspects of his nature.[12] He is conscious on the one hand of his animal instincts which limit him to a place in the physical, biological world but is aware also on the other hand of his capacity to reason which enables him to transcend the animal realm and gives him a certain responsible freedom. It is the uncertainty engendered by the conflict of his double nature and the continuing question as to what he really is which gives rise in man to anxiety.[13] Here is Rabbit's situation exactly. He is emphatically a biological creature (note the nickname itself) given to irrational impulses and strong appetites. The physical acts and reacts upon him in most elementary fashion. A sound, sight, taste, or touch can provoke a sudden reflex which he himself does not wholly understand. At the same time he is profoundly, almost neurotically, sensitive and self-conscious. He struggles to rise above his drives and impulses and is miserable when he cannot. The tension between the two sides of himself causes the anxiety that Niebuhr describes. In Rabbit's case the anxiety often takes the form of panic. His experiences in the novel are in fact nothing more than cycles of impulses, moments of self-awareness, dissatisfaction, and resultant panic. The first flight away from Mt. Judge, when he heads for the South, is fraught with panic; the novel ends on the same note, as he breaks away from the graveyard ceremony and then, refused by Ruth, runs out of desperation: "with an effortless gathering out of a kind of sweet panic growing lighter and quicker and quieter, he runs. Ah: runs. Runs" (255).

Man without grace, according to Niebuhr, can turn in either of two directions: to a retreat into his animal nature or to a false faith in his rationality.

When anxiety has conceived it brings forth both pride and sensuality. Man falls into pride, when he seeks to raise his contingent

12. *Nature*, I, 1.
13. *Ibid.*, pp. 1 ff. Cf. also I, 82: "In short, man, being both free and bound, both limited and limitless, is anxious. Anxiety is the inevitable concomitant of the paradox of freedom and finiteness in which man is involved."

19

existence to unconditioned significance; he falls into sensuality, when he seeks to escape from his unlimited possibilities of freedom, from the perils and responsibilities of self-determination.[14]

Rabbit stumbles into both. Niebuhr shows how pride expresses itself in the pride of power and glory, intellectual pride, moral pride, and religious pride.[15] Rabbit is guilty of them all. His pride of power and glory finds expression, for example, in his desire to recapture the attention of the crowds that he enjoyed as a basketball hero. His intellectual pride reveals itself in his contempt for the customers he cons into buying cheap products and in his lightly disguised disgust at his wife's brainlessness. His moral pride is built up at the expense of Ruth, his mistress, while spiritual pride comes to the fore in the smugness with which he considers the quality of his Lutheran Christianity. All of these are for Rabbit (as Niebuhr states in general terms) really attempts to cover his fundamental insecurity. In the last analysis, he is unable to rely on reputation, intellect, moral stature, or religion, so that in nurturing each of them he is only practicing self-deception.

More immediately apparent is Rabbit's retreat into sensuality, which finds its main (although not its exclusive) expression in sexuality. Niebuhr points out the paradox of the individual seeking escape in sexuality; he is pressing self-love to the limit and simultaneously seeking a way out of the trap of self-love by sharing himself with another.[16] Rabbit is caught pathetically in the trap. Note the initial bedroom scene with Ruth, in which "he makes love to her as he would to his wife" (71). Rabbit wants a whore to indulge and satisfy his sexual appetite. Indeed, at first meeting they even dislike each other. At the same time, he is appalled at her matter-of-factness regarding intercourse and wants to make love to her not mechanically but spiritually.

The same contradiction leads to the final alienating argument between Rabbit and Janice in the acutely embarrassing scene (for both the participants and the reader) a few days after Janice returns home from the maternity ward. Rabbit needs sexual relief, but he also wants to share himself with his wife after the long estrangement. When she rejects him, Rabbit leaves, frustrated not only in

14. *Ibid.*, p. 186.
15. *Ibid.*, pp. 186-203.
16. *Ibid.*, pp. 237 ff.

his physical passion but above all in feeling the loss of some re-discovered part of himself:

For what made him mad at Janice wasn't so much that she was in the right for once and he was wrong and stupid but the closed feeling of it, the feeling of being closed in. He had gone to church and brought back this little flame and had nowhere to put it on the dark damp walls of the apartment, so it had flickered and gone out. . . . What held him back all day was the feeling that somewhere there was something better for him than listening to babies cry and cheating people in used-car lots (225).

Rabbit is "closed in" because he has closed himself in. The escape from sensuality through sexuality will not work. Instead, Rabbit experiences three other things that Niebuhr relates to autonomous sex: sex as shame; sex as nothingness; and sex as subconscious existence. Both Janice and Ruth are ashamed of their bodies and of themselves when involved in the sexual act with Rabbit. The reason for that sort of shame, says Niebuhr, is the instinctive awareness of a passion that has been divorced from the transcendent.[17] Thus it is not surprising that the relationship of Ruth and Rabbit comes to an end when he forces her to a perverted act which defines her position as a prostitute and kills whatever genuine love may have been between them (175).

Also, notes Niebuhr, sex can "serve as an anodyne. The ego, having found the worship both of self and of the other abortive, may use the passion of sex, without reference to self and the other, as a form of escape from the tension of life. . . . It is a flight not to a false god but to nothingness."[18] That is Rabbit's feeling. He has sought out Ruth as a means of distracting himself from the ruins of his marriage, but even the moment of greatest passion with her is accompanied by his sense of futility:

He looks in her face and seems to read in its shadows a sad expression of forgiveness, as if she knows that at the moment of release, the root of love, he betrayed her by feeling despair. Nature leads you up like a mother and as soon as she gets her little price leaves you with nothing (73).

All sensuality, then, from fondling a basketball to lusting after a woman, is for Rabbit "finally an effort to escape from the con-

17. *Ibid.*   18. *Ibid.*, p. 237.

21

fusion which sin has created into some form of subconscious existence."[19] Rabbit's running at the close of the novel becomes a profound metaphor. The running itself is subconsciously motivated, begins of its own accord (255), and the sheer physicality of it becomes the way out when he dare no longer plan or think.

Rabbit's tragedy (and although he is not individually big enough, he is representative enough to be tragic) is that, unlike Cass Kinsolving, his crisis does not lead to redemption. The real indictment of the American Protestant society which Updike treats is its failure to give Rabbit a saving answer. There is little doubt that Rabbit's predicament is a religious one or that Updike considers it such. The quotation from Pascal preceding the novel speaks of "the motions of Grace, the hardness of the heart; external circumstances." In that sentence are embodied the three aspects of Niebuhr's analysis, two of which we have been discussing: individual sin ("the hardness of the heart") and social evil ("external circumstances"). The other, "the motions of Grace," is also evident throughout the book, but Rabbit cannot find grace because the term itself has become hackneyed and because the context of Rabbit's Protestantism will not admit the seriousness of sin from which grace can result.[20]

Nevertheless, Rabbit's search is a search for God. Updike sketches skillfully the outlines of Rabbit's pathetic religious mentality. "Both are Christians," he writes of Rabbit and Janice (12), but it is a naïve faith that responds to the ridiculous sermons of Jimmy the Mouseketeer on television. Still, it is a faith that includes an elementary sense of guilt. "God's name makes them feel guilty" (12). On the Sunday morning after the first night with Ruth, Rabbit prays:

19. *Ibid.*, p. 240.
20. Ward, I think, mistakes Updike's description of the shallow Protestant mentality for Updike's own view. He writes, "True, there are some vague and scattered longings for God (Rabbit likes the looks of people going to churches), but neither the official explanations of the minister nor Rabbit's own puzzled gropings leads anywhere. In a world-view that negates reason, epistemology and theology can be only absurd." And: "As a criticism of life, *Rabbit, Run* is marred not so much by its sympathetic view of irresponsibility and retreat as by its implied denial that man is a rational and social animal" (p. 35). A knowledge of neo-orthodoxy and of Updike's relation to it would have prevented Ward from rendering those judgments. Updike, like Niebuhr, does not negate reason nor deny that man is a social animal. He does say, albeit negatively, that reason is not enough for man to solve his problems of existence and shows that Rabbit's problem is in locating the missing third dimension—the transcendent.

Help me, Christ. Forgive me. Take me down the way. Bless Ruth, Janice, Nelson, my mother and father, Mr. and Mrs. Springer, and the unborn baby. Forgive Tothero and all the others. Amen (77).

And during Janice's labor he is terrified that she will die as divine punishment for his sins (164). Rabbit wants to get beyond the confines of his traditional Lutheranism and tries to articulate his longing to Eccles, the minister: "Well I don't know about all this theology, but I'll tell you. I *do* feel, I guess, that somewhere behind all this . . . there's something that wants me to find it" (107). Eccles cannot help him, nor can Kruppenbach, Rabbit's own pastor. Eccles has enough trouble with his own faith and, in fact, confesses to his wife, "If it'll make you happy, I don't believe in anything" (223), while old Kruppenbach has already labeled Rabbit a *Schussel* (Pennsylvania German for a no-good) and insists to Eccles that the only thing to do is pray (143).

The final experience that might have saved Rabbit also fails. When his daughter dies, Rabbit feels the remorse he should and moves toward repentance. He wants a solid basis for a new life of responsibility and pleads with Eccles for it. And even though Eccles rejects him (234), Rabbit has the religious experience briefly at the graveyard ceremony, but loses it when the others present cannot understand him. Listening to the burial service, hoping desperately that his daughter will go to heaven, Rabbit feels an exultant momentary faith. He wants to forgive and be forgiven, but in trying to make things "straight," he meets only the hostility of the others (234 f.) and flees. Rabbit's kind of experience is described by Niebuhr. "The fact of responsibility is attested by the feeling of remorse or repentance which follows the sinful action."[21] The ultimate step would be the recognition and acceptance of God's grace and forgiveness, the *agape* love which accepts what is unacceptable. Rabbit has begun to feel that love, but since it can exist only in the reciprocation of the community, and since Rabbit's community does not possess it, he loses it at once. The possibility of freedom from pride and sensuality briefly opened to him becomes again a vacuum into which confusion and then panic re-enter.

Just before his final evening flight, Rabbit sees the church:

Afraid, really afraid, he remembers what once consoled him by seeming to make a hole where he looked through into underlying

21. Niebuhr, *Nature*, p. 255.

brightness, and lifts his eyes to the church window. It is, because of church poverty or the late summer nights or just carelessness, unlit, a dark circle in a stone façade (254).

Rabbit has lost what faith he had. He has failed himself because his community has failed him. The force of Updike's novel, like Niebuhr's theology, is in exposing a society which, because it will not come to terms with its evil, cannot find the redemption of love.

4. PHILIP ROTH AND THE TEST OF DIALOGIC LIFE

Philip Roth's concern with ethical behavior is a natural reflection of his Jewish background. It follows likewise that his religious interest is, if anything, still easier to establish than that of Styron and Updike. His first book, the novelette *Goodbye, Columbus,* as well as most of his *New Yorker* short stories, treats religion seriously, and one critic, in fact, was ready to place Roth at the age of twenty-six in the company of modern Jewish moralists.[1] Moreover, Roth has worked previously and well with the theme of the religious crisis. Both "The Conversion of the Jews" and "Eli, the Fanatic," for example, center on such a crisis. In *Letting Go,* Roth's fiction takes on a dimension and an orientation hitherto lacking.[2] There he explores the human condition from an angle which tempers the Jewish heritage with the existential thought of Martin Buber. The question of Roth's deeper acquaintance with Buber's philosophy must of course remain open, although he does have the protagonist mention Buber and his contemporary relevance in *Goodbye, Columbus.*[3] I hope to show that in *Letting Go,* Roth's presentation of the burdening involvements which the protagonist-narrator experiences and which bring on his breakdown receives particular significance when interpreted in the light of and tested against Buber's concept of personal and superpersonal encounter.

Letting Go even more than *Rabbit, Run* is a story of human relationships, but there is a fundamental difference between the two. Updike writes of relationships (in the plural) and describes connections between individuals and natural and social institutions as symptomatic of the individual and societal search for God. Roth writes of relationship (in the singular) as both the method of and the place for finding ultimate meaning.

Letting Go is the story of, and is told mainly by, Gabriel Wallach, young Jewish English professor, but it is just as much the story of

1. Theodore Solotaroff, "Philip Roth and the Jewish Moralists," *Chicago Review,* XIII (Winter, 1959), 87-99.
2. Quotations are from *Letting Go,* by Philip Roth. ©Copyright 1962 by Philip Roth. Reprinted by permission of Random House, Inc. Page numbers immediately follow quotations from the text.
3. Roth, *Goodbye, Columbus* (Boston: Houghton Mifflin, 1959), p. 88.

the people in whose lives he becomes involved and entangled. The involvements begin with Paul and Libby Herz, a Jewish graduate student and the gentile wife he met at the University of Iowa while finishing his own doctoral program there. The Herzes are poor, Libby is sickly and neurotic, their marriage is unhappy. Gabe, supported by a wealthy dentist father in New York, is drawn into performing some favors for the Herzes and in the process falls uncertainly in love with Libby.

From that point onward Gabe's life becomes a matter, often involuntary, of helping the Herzes. After the Iowa sojourn, Gabe takes a teaching position at the University of Chicago and finds a job there for Paul Herz (now in Pennsylvania) also. He tries to heal the estrangement between Paul and his parents in Brooklyn brought on by Paul's marriage to a gentile, and finally, when Paul and Libby decide that an adopted child would help both her and their marriage (she has had one abortion; poor health prevents a second pregnancy), Gabe is the one who tries to arrange a private adoption. He brings them a daughter, the illegitimate baby of Theresa, a young, married Catholic girl, but encounters the stubbornness of Theresa's husband in trying to make the adoption legal without involving the Herzes. After trying threats and bribes with only partial success, Gabe, who is baby-sitting for the Herzes, takes the child back to Theresa and her husband in an attempt to engage their sympathy. In the ensuing argument, the already overwrought Gabe collapses, frightening the pair into finally giving up the child. The Herzes get their daughter, but Gabe leaves Chicago and travels to Europe. The novel ends with a letter from Gabe to Libby severing connections between them.

In addition to the Herzes, Gabe has other painful relationships and liaisons in the novel. He is plagued by his lately widowed father in New York, who pursues the son with a pathetic overlove and possessiveness. He has a brief interlude with Marge Howells, a coed at Iowa, who moves in with him for a month and becomes his "Bartleby." Theresa briefly mistakes his intentions, and, most grueling of all, in Chicago he enters a frustrating affair with Martha Regenhart, a divorcee with two children. All the relations proceed in essence like the one with Libby and Paul. Marge moves out of the Iowa apartment claiming she has been "used." Old Wallach marries a semialcoholic widow and affects a new detached attitude toward his son. Martha is untrue to him even in their unmarried agreement and finally marries a persistent suitor. Gabe is left alone in the end with a breakdown and estranged from all those he loved or respected.

Although Buber's philosophy, unlike the theology of Tillich and Niebuhr, is not programmatic, there are certain points of emphasis in his thought which one can apply to Roth's novel in order to demonstrate the affinity between them. In most general terms, one can define Buber's central concern as located in the concept of relation. In the resumé of *Letting Go* I indicated the importance of relation and the multiplicity of relationships which arise. The next step is to show how those relationships reflect a specific attitude, shared by Buber and Roth, regarding the human situation, and receive ultimate religious meaning. Buber's definition of man's twofold attitude, described in his famous "primary words" of *I-Thou* and *I-It*, can serve as a basis for understanding the novel. "All real living is meeting," says Buber.[4] That meeting is what Buber has in mind when he speaks of I-Thou. It is the direct encounter of one person, in his "whole being," with the whole being of another. Buber refuses to call the encounter an experience or even a feeling. It is a complete meeting, simply that. Contrasted with it is the I-It, which refers to man's usual relationship to his world and to his fellows. I-It is characterized by a certain detachment, by an interest in things, by the activities of experiencing and using. While recognizing the necessity of I-It for human existence, Buber places it on a lower plane than I-Thou and maintains that man finds his meaning only in I-Thou.

In *Letting Go*, Gabe Wallach and his fellows are engaged in a search for the I-Thou while existing in the unsatisfying involvements of I-It. A troublesome characteristic of the I in the I-It relationship is its propensity to use, to make objects. In some situations that is good, but it becomes demonic when applied to persons, when the I transforms the Thou of the other person to an It: "In the I-It posture the 'I' holds back—measuring, using, and even seeking to control the object of its attention—but never, as in the I-Thou relation, affirming the other just as it is in itself."[5]

4. Martin Buber, *I and Thou*. Translated by Ronald Gregor Smith (New York: Charles Scribner's Sons, 1958), p. 11. All quotations by permission of the publisher.
5. Malcolm L. Diamond, *Martin Buber: Jewish Existentialist* (New York: Oxford University Press, 1960), pp. 21-22. All quotations by permission of the publisher.

27

Letting Go begins with an example of the I-It attitude, opening with a deathbed letter to Gabe from his mother, in which she confesses to a subtle manipulation of people throughout her life:

Since I was a little girl I always wanted to be Very Decent to People. . . . I was always doing things for another's good. The rest of my life I could push or pull at people with a clear conscience (2).

Gabe seems to have inherited the attribute of decency from his mother, for like her, he constantly does things for the good of others. He pleases his father, he yields to Marge Howells, he aids the Herzes, he comforts Martha Regenhart, he rescues Theresa when she has her bastard child. But in none of these instances does he really confront the others with his whole self nor does he look for them in their fullness. Toward his father he feels duty and filial love but guards against overinvolvement. Toward Marge and Martha he experiences desire but stays away, as far as possible, from specific commitments. He cannot meet Libby on honest grounds because he is infatuated with her; he cannot face Paul truly because he is Libby's husband. Theresa he pities but uses nonetheless. In all of these situations there is certainly a mutual fault. Gabe's failing is always either the initiation or reflex of a failing by the other individual. Thus he reacts against the possessiveness of his father and of Marge Howells, reacts instinctively against the secret jealousy of Paul Herz. He cannot really meet Martha, even though he lives with her, because she doesn't want to meet him; and finally, he cannot know Libby because of her neurotic preoccupation with herself.

What makes all the relationships especially difficult is that Gabe senses that there should be more to them but cannot change them. Once he nearly meets his father on the dialogic basis. Home from Iowa for the Christmas holidays, he sits in the dentist chair while his father cleans his teeth and harasses him with petty complaints. In the midst of it Gabe suddenly understands his father's baffled love for him and almost responds:

Then his face appeared above my own. I could have reached up and pulled him down and kissed him. But would he understand that I was not prepared to surrender my life to his? He was a wholehearted man, and such people are hard to kiss half-heartedly (39).

Later, when Gabe and Paul Herz are both on the Chicago faculty, they do experience a fleeting I-Thou encounter. They have been talking formally, although behind the conversation the awareness of Libby holds both of them. It is the closest they come to verbalizing the tension between them, and when Paul mentions his wife, the honesty of the moment draws them together, even though the subject is precisely the one that separates them. Gabe says, "I don't think it would have shocked either of us then if we had embraced. It was the kind of emotional moment that one knows is being shared" (240).

But these moments are seldom. Mostly, Gabe does what Buber claims is the essence of the I-It. He experiences and uses people.[6] He and Marge live together casually for a month and more, congratulating themselves at first for the sophisticated arrangement, but the breakup is accompanied by accusations. "You *used* me, you bastard," Marge tells him (41). Gabe is the realist. "The truth is we were both used. We used each other" (40). And that is the problem of Gabe's life and of the lives of his friends. They want to share themselves and to encounter the other person, but they always end up employing the other person to their own ends. "Every *Thou* in the world is by its nature fated to become a thing, or continually to re-enter into the condition of things," says Buber.[7] For Gabe, the others become objectified according to his needs and desires, their Thou becomes It; while to the others Gabe is also a means to their end. It is no accident that *Letting Go* is almost all dialogue or narration by the protagonist. The incessant conversation represents the attempt to find and speak the "primary words" of I-Thou which forever lose themselves in the description and analysis of things.

Buber turns repeatedly to the marriage relationship as the ideal expression of I-Thou, in which each person shares himself unselfishly but grows through the encounter. Buber rejects the concept of union as the marriage ideal and emphasizes the importance of what takes place *between* the partners instead. "The heart of marriage, as of love, is in responding to the other within a framework created by the relationship itself."[8] Roth also employs marriage as a means of exhibiting the problems of true relation. Nearly as much as the story of Gabe Wallach's search for real encounter, *Letting Go* is the narrative of the marriage of Paul and Libby Herz. In fact, it is the marital difficulty which often involves Gabe, and the love

6. Cf. Buber, pp. 34, 38.   7. *Ibid.*, p. 17.
8. Diamond, p. 28. Cf. also Buber, pp. 98 f.

that exists for a time between Gabe and Libby is a result rather than the original cause of the difficulty.

The interfaith marriage is in trouble from the start. It causes the estrangement from parents on both sides; it suffers from poverty, then from sexual maladjustment.

But the root of the matter is the spiritual quandary. Paul and Libby never encounter each other. Paul is absorbed in the Jewishness of his background, in his profession, in his pride; Libby has false ideas about giving herself "wholeheartedly" to Paul and experiences guilt when she cannot. For both of them marriage is a self-conscious effort that hinders the recognition and appreciation of the other in his entirety. Paul's one-afternoon dalliance with Marge Howells, his deliberate attempt to throw Gabe and Libby together, his brief separation from Libby, all indicate defensive stratagems to force an objective I-It relation where the I-Thou has failed. "You see, we're not one person. We're two," says Libby wistfully toward the end of the novel (614), and in that statement reflects not only an impossible marriage ideal but the incipient step toward a possible solution. For up to this point Paul and Libby have suffered under the illusion of marriage as union. Libby tries to subject her life completely to Paul's and cannot; Paul tries to guide Libby's life, make it conform to his, meanwhile rebelling against the idea of sharing himself. The realization of their twoness is at least a release from illusion and the basis for a start in the right direction. The Thou, says Buber, "teaches you to meet others, and to hold your ground when you meet them."[9] That assertion of individuality while participating in the life of the other is what Paul and Libby need.

The other marriages in the novel also underscore, in their negative aspects, the necessity for genuine encounter. The marriage of Martha and Dick Regenhart failed because of extreme egotism. The marriage of Gabe's father to Fay Silberman is a pathetic maneuver to overcome loneliness. Mrs. Silberman is "a good-time Charley," but hardly the partner that the sensitive Dr. Wallach needs. Maury and Doris Horvitz, Paul's friends, have a middle-class marriage: casual and regular sex, acquired cultural tastes, and a suspicion of anyone who hints that they might not be happy. Finally, Gabe's own affair with Martha ends with the discovery that the *eros* is not enough to sustain a relationship, no matter how well-defined its limits were at the start.

9. Buber, p. 33.

The I-Thou encounter is so important for Buber because out of it emerges the encounter with the "eternal Thou," the God of Buber's faith. The encounter itself must be the basis for one's relationship with God, because doctrine and dogma about God are only a part of the I-It situation which appeal to the intellect but cannot satisfy one's total need. Thus Buber rejects objective criteria in discussing the religious experience (neither "religious" nor "experience" according to Buber's redefinitions) in favor of the existential "passionate engagement."[10] "Human truth can be communicated only when one throws one's self into the process and answers for it with one's self."[11] *Letting Go* shares Buber's unconcern for religious dogma and in fact gently ridicules the answers of traditional faiths to man's search for God. Beyond that, Roth follows Buber in his presentation of Paul Herz's "revelation" and of Gabe's breakdown. From both comes an existential encounter with meaning and reality that supersedes normal religious experience and which determines the future action of the character.

Libby's religious preoccupation is the most overt manifestation of religious concern in the novel; at the same time, her experiences are the least profound, and Roth uses her and her situation to satirize the traditional positions. Libby has been raised a Catholic; she has "a past full of Gloriful Heaven and Sweet Jesus" (143). The letter she receives from her father (in response to a request for money), urging her to seek an annulment of her marriage in the interests of "the Shining Light" is a model of religious bigotry (141-42). Libby's attempts to assume Jewishness, in turn, make both herself and her new faith look foolish.[12] She undergoes the *mikvah* bath in her "old blue Jantzen" swimsuit; later, having tried a psychiatrist with little success, she is temporarily calmed by *The Wonder of Life,* a book subtitled "Suggestions for the Jewish Homemaker" (353).

Perhaps there was one final way out of all this mess that was not psychoanalysis, or money in the bank, or carnality, or self-pity, or madness: Religion. . . . not a belief in God necessarily . . . *traditions and ceremonies, holy days and holidays and customs* (353).

10. Diamond, p. 19.
11. Reprinted by permission of Schocken Books, Inc. from *Israel and the World, Essays in a Time of Crisis* by Martin Buber, p. 46. (Second edition) ©Copyright 1948, 1963, by Schocken Books, Inc.
12. Roth got in his licks against Protestantism early in the description of the affair between Gabe and Marge Howells (27).

Yet hardly an hour later she is in wildest hysterics. Similarly, one cannot take seriously her later talks with Paul and Gabe about religion. Libby has become religious, but religion has done nothing for her.

Paul and Gabe undergo something more profound. Paul's crisis begins when the news of his father's dying reaches him. His trip to his estranged parents in Brooklyn is also a flight from Libby but turns into a confrontation with himself. There he faces his two problems: his Jewishness and his relationship with Libby. He will not go to his father's deathbed and when the father dies, Paul remains in rebellion against his background and his wife. Instead of attending the funeral he determines to locate a job in New York that will keep him free of Libby and his relatives. Yet he is drawn to the graveyard in spite of himself, and once there, the atmosphere of death leads him to ponder his own mortality. In true existential fashion the knowledge that he must die by himself makes him aware that he must also live by himself, so that he is forced into the awareness of his own ultimate responsibility.[13] Neither his parents nor his race nor his wife can live for him. He meets his relatives in the cemetery and the moment of reconciliation with his mother there becomes the moment of freedom also:

For his truth was revealed to him, his final premise melted away. What he had taken for order was chaos. Justice was illusion. Abraham and Isaac were one. His eyes opened, and in the midst of those faces—the faces of his dream, the faces of the bums, all the faces that had forever encircled him—he felt no humiliation and no shame. Their eyes no longer overpowered him. He felt himself under a wider beam (451).

What makes Paul's "revelation," his encounter with reality, different from, say, the existential moment of Kierkegaard, is that it like Buber's takes place within and through the "community." Paul

13. It is no accident, I think, that Roth relates Paul's crisis to the story of Abraham and Isaac, the same example that Kierkegaard employed to explain existential faith. Paul sees the grave of a child named Abrams, born the same year as himself, and connects it with the Old Testament story. Paul's crisis is existential with the coloring of Buber's thought. He is forced by the pressure of life to reflect upon himself; he enters a critical period of extreme doubt and anguish; he is moved by the awareness of death to ponder the meaning of life; he is brought through a kind of grace to a moment of decision, and in that decision he loosens himself from the hindrances of the past and achieves freedom.

32

finds his freedom and understands his responsibility only as he achieves the reconciliation with his Jewish relatives and friends. It is the human I-Thou meeting which leads Paul to an encounter with the eternal Thou. Roth's treatment of the encounter is further like Buber's in his reluctance to provide an objective description of the God whom Paul has met.[14] Roth writes only, "He felt himself under a wider beam" (451). Later, Paul refuses to discuss the nature of his God with Libby on her terms not because he doesn't want to, but because he cannot (614 ff.). Yet, since his crisis in the cemetery, Paul has returned to Libby against his previous plans and has at least tried to establish a mutuality with her that approaches the I-Thou relation. Paul's response to the eternal Thou leads him to want to meet his wife in her "subjectivity," and that, for Buber as well as for Roth, would be the best indication of existential encounter that one could wish.[15]

Gabe's crisis, which brings the events to a climax, is like Paul's in its existential orientation but different in the attitudes precipitating it. Libby's response to the demands of reality was a neurotic flight to various "solutions," the last of which was therapeutic religion. Paul indulged the stoic pose, suffering silently the misunderstanding of relatives and friends (and vaguely enjoying it), until he was forced to face himself in the death of his father and the separation from his wife. Gabe is plagued by indecision, a genuine paralysis of the will that determines his involvement in the lives of others more than do any altruistic designs. It is a dangerous involvement, since it gives Gabe responsibilities he cannot handle. Behind it all is Gabe's confusion about who and what he should be. He is guilty about his wealth and independence and feels obligated to help others, but since helping others puts them in an objective relationship to him, he never meets the others in the I-Thou.[16] He sees his father as the grieving widower, Paul as the poor academician, Libby as the frustrated wife, Martha as the wronged divorcee, all of them categorized and in need of a special aid that he should give them. Worse still, Gabe is as unsure as the others about his motives, so that the help he offers has a suspicious flavor. Instead of the passionate engagement, Gabe's approach is

14. Diamond, pp. 46, 51.   15. Buber, *I and Thou*, p. 62.
16. Cf. Buber, *Between Man and Man* (London: Routledge and Kegan Paul, Ltd., 1947), p. 16: "Genuine responsibility exists only where there is real responding."

one of hesitation, of letting things happen, and in letting them happen he, inadvertently, becomes the manipulator that his mother was and that Spigliano, the despised department head, is.

Buber speaks to Gabe's problem in *I and Thou*, when he says, "Causality has an unlimited reign in the world of *It*."[17] He shows that where genuine human relationship is lacking, the objective forces of life will take over, and he condemns indecision as the human evil which allows the world of It to predominate.[18] In Gabe's life, the failure to establish relation becomes catastrophic. Gabe's father remarries unwisely in a reaction against Gabe's lack of understanding; Gabe's connections with the Herzes become more and more strained; his liaison with Martha evolves into a mutual hate. Not until the moment when Gabe finally makes the decision that forces encounter, in which he at last bares himself, do matters change. The result is Gabe's breakdown, but it is also his introduction to a new life. The crisis comes in the scene when Gabe, making a final desperate attempt to legalize the adoption of the Herz's child, becomes involved in the argument which emotionally shatters him.

The effects of the experience upon Gabe are revealed in his letter to Libby at the novel's conclusion. Gabe cherishes his moment of decision even though it brought him a breakdown:

If you've lived for a long while as an indecisive man, you can't simply forget, obliterate, bury, your one decisive moment. I can't—in the name of the future, perhaps—accept forgiveness for my time of strength, even if that time was so very brief, and was followed . . . by the dissolution of character, of everything (630).

Like Paul Herz, Gabe has learned the meaning of responsibility to himself. The failure of the I-It relationships has forced him to look beyond them, to search for the encounter of the Thou in others. In cutting himself off from Libby now he is not acting selfishly but truthfully; he is taking the initial step of dissolving the I-It relation that has plagued his life and the lives of his friends. More significant, the crisis has led him to seek the eternal Thou. Gabe has not been religious in the traditional sense at all; yet the final words of the book are his confession to Libby:

It is only kind of you, Libby, to feel that I would want to know that I am off the hook. But I'm not, I can't be, I don't even want to be—not until I make some sense of the larger hook I'm on (630).

17. Buber, *I and Thou*, p. 51.   18. *Ibid.*, p. 52.

Gabe has assumed a new kind of responsibility, to learn to live in the encounter with reality, and that, in Buber's terms, makes his crisis and his future life religious.[19]

The provocative title, *Letting Go,* I submit, does not refer to Gabe's ultimate rejection of responsibility toward others in favor of a self-preservation, as it might at first seem. That would be too cheap for Roth. It means a release from the egotistical instinct that uses others, a "letting go" of one's grasp of the objective life in favor of true encounter. One critic of Roth, in comparing him with Bernard Malamud, gives a thoughtful summary of what happens to Roth's characters. He speaks of the "conversion into the essential Jew, achieved by acts of striving, sacrificing, and suffering for the sake of some fundamental goodness and truth in one's self that has been lost and buried. Further, both Roth and Malamud emphasize the vague, semi-conscious character of the decision, proceeding not from any clear idea but rather from awakening feelings of sympathy, love, identification, and guilt which, becoming more and more powerful, finally indicate their purpose—to produce the suffering and sacrifice that lead to purification and to a discovery of one's true identity."[20] He could have said it more simply in Buber's terms: "The person becomes conscious of himself as sharing in being, as co-existing, and thus as being."[21] By "letting go," Gabe has changed his life, and as Buber puts it, "the event that from the side of the world is called turning is called from God's side redemption."[22]

19. Buber, *Between Man and Man,* p. 14.
20. Solotaroff, pp. 92-93.
21. Buber, *I and Thou,* p. 63.
22. *Ibid.,* p. 120.

5. J. D. SALINGER AND THE
QUEST FOR SAINTHOOD

A study dealing with the individual religious experience cannot ignore that most discussed of crises in recent American fiction, namely, Franny Glass's slightly suspect nervous breakdown in Salinger's *Franny and Zooey*.[1] Salinger even more than Roth appears fascinated by the individual crisis and particularly by the crisis that has religious origin or result.[2] Holden Caulfield's trouble in *The Catcher in the Rye* has been given theological interpretation;[3] in later stories we learn that the suicide of Seymour Glass ("A Perfect Day for Bananafish") had religious connotations, as did the quasi-breakdown of Sergeant X in "For Esme—with Love and Squalor."

Unlike the other three authors discussed, Salinger cannot be interpreted in terms of a specific theological position. He reflects instead a typically American religious attitude which, at odds with the traditional creeds and swept by winds of doctrine, fashions a faith from pieces of popular movements. Speaking for the Glasses in the novel at hand, Zooey points out emphatically the diversity of religious conviction in his family (153).[4] The gospel of Seymour is informed by Christianity (Protestant, Catholic, mystic varieties), a large dose of Zen Buddhism, a smattering of existential terminology, and a flavoring of Jewish tradition.[5] Although I do not think that

1. J. D. Salinger, *Franny and Zooey* (London: William Heineman, Ltd., 1962). Since Mr. Salinger has refused permission to use quotations from his story, the page numbers in the text refer the reader to relevant portions of dialogue.
2. In fact, at the beginning of *Zooey* (48-49), Salinger has the narrator discuss the difficulties of using the name "God" in fiction.
3. Nathan A. Scott, Jr., *Modern Literature and the Religious Frontier* (New York: Harper & Row, 1958), pp. 90 ff. All quotations by permission of the publisher.
4. The Glasses themselves embody the religious heterogeneity. Les Glass, the father, is Jewish, while Mrs. Glass is Irish Catholic, and Waker, a son, is a Catholic priest. Seymour and Buddy were absorbed in Eastern mysticism, particularly in Zen, but also fascinated by existentialism of the Kierkegaardian variety. Cf. *Raise High the Roofbeam, Carpenters,* and *Seymour—An Introduction* (Boston: Little, Brown & Co., 1963).
5. Considering the Jewish flavoring, I am surprised that no one has yet connected the pilgrim of Franny's Jesus Prayer with the holy men of Hasidism, Buber's original source of religious inspiration. The parallels are striking. *Hasid* itself means "a pious one." Like the Jesus Prayer movement,

the net result as applied to Franny's problem is altogether convincing, the following analysis should at least demonstrate once more the central religious concern of a popularly received "secular" novel and should underscore the significance of religion as a serious consideration in our latest fiction.

The plot of *Franny and Zooey*, such as it is, can be sketched in a few sentences. In the forty-odd pages of *Franny*, Franny Glass, youngest of the Glass geniuses and a college coed, has a mild nervous breakdown in a restaurant with her date at the beginning of a big Yale football week end. The illness is provoked mainly by Franny's reading a small book about a Russian pilgrim and the Jesus Prayer. In *Zooey*, about three times as long, Franny is at the parental Glass apartment in New York nursing the collapse. Zooey, next oldest Glass and a television actor, has a discussion about his sister with Bessie (the Glass mother) in the bathroom, and then two sessions with Franny herself in which he half talks, half tricks her out of her emotional and religious crisis.

Franny's underlying difficulty, the fundamental cause of her breakdown, is not just that she is disgusted by her own ego (29) or overcome by phoniness, although these are her initial complaints. The crisis, long in coming, is the result of a confused concept of sainthood. As one learns in the epistle of Buddy to Zooey, written on the third anniversary of Seymour's suicide (56-69), Zooey and Franny were subjected as children by Seymour and Buddy to regular doses of mysticism, Oriental and Western. Believing in the direct confrontation with reality, the ecstatic experience, the two elder brothers wished to tutor the younger children in the doctrines of the mystics (65). Buddy's letter, in fact, lists the names of the masters, ranging from Christ and Buddha and Ramakrishna down to Blake and Whitman.

The sessions on metaphysics were apparently successful; at least both Zooey and Franny learned from them a certain aloofness from things that contributed to the contemplative life and a reverence

Hasidism began in eastern Europe (Poland) in small villages and spread through Russia. According to Franny, the Jesus Prayer movement took place during the 1800's; the early phase of Hasidism was from c. 1750-1825. The founder of Hasidism, Israel Ben Eliezer, was known as the Baal Shem Tov, "Master of the Good Name," reminiscent of the pilgrim's concern in Franny's book with the name of God. Most important, both movements stressed holy living through a direct encounter with God and coupled that holiness with a desire to transform the community as well.

for the omnipresent supernatural. The trauma occurred with Seymour's suicide, the death of the saint in the Glass household. Seymour's death is the blow from which the Glass children have never recovered. They suffer the incongruity of his great vision and the apparent self-betrayal of his suicide.[6] Buddy was able to stand the shock; Zooey was also far enough along to hold up, but Franny, thirteen at the time, had her faith shaken and damaged. Buddy admits his failure to come to her aid in the year following Seymour's death (he was ashamed and afraid to) and worries about her (66-67). And rightly so, for Franny's frustrated attachment to Seymour is obvious. The two pilgrim books which are the immediate cause of her breakdown she has taken from Seymour's room, now a holy place and generally taboo for casual entry. Most indicative of all, when Zooey asks her, in the midst of her breakdown, if a long distance call to Buddy would help, Franny replies that she wants to talk to Seymour. In her devotion to her older brother, Franny reveals a false conception of sainthood that infects her total religious perspective. She becomes obsessed with the idea of *imitatio* instead of *revelatio* and through the mechanics of the Jesus Prayer intends to force the ecstasy, the *satori*, or whatever label one cares to give the mystic experience.

Zooey's response is to enlighten her on two scores. The first is that the encounter with reality cannot be coerced by a semimagical conditioning of one's own spiritual reflexes, via, in this instance, the constant repetition of the pilgrim's petition. The second is that the unmediated experience of reality does not take place divorced from daily life but precisely through one's intercourse with society.[7] Zooey does not disenchant his sister of the Jesus Prayer; he simply shows her (granted rather rudely) that the formula will not work if it is geared to the wrong power, and Franny's prayer is, in fact, directed more to her dead brother than to Christ (168). Following the pattern of the pilgrim in the little book, Franny is looking desperately for an East-West mystic to teach her how to use the prayer, in order to experience a direct encounter with reality (112). Her

6. Ihab Hassam in "The Casino of Silence," *Saturday Review* (January 26, 1963), p. 38, says, "Seymour haunts all the Glasses. . . . His example is the cross they bear and his suicide the event for which they must atone."
7. This last, of course, is Suzuki's influence. He insists upon the daily Nirvana, experiencing God in the here and now and through the "suchness" of all aspects of life. Cf. Daisetz Teitaro Suzuki, *Living by Zen* (London: Rider Press, 1950), pp. 49, 136.

frustration stems from the fact that Seymour, who should be her teacher, is dead, but in his death he has become her surrogate for Jesus. Franny's *imitatio* is thus of the pilgrim but also of Seymour; her dead end lies in her identification of Seymour the saint with Seymour as the quintessence of sainthood, namely, as an incarnation of ultimate reality. Zooey becomes Franny's guru, and in showing her the right use and meaning of the Jesus Prayer, also helps her place Seymour in proper focus. He explains to her that the aim of the Jesus Prayer is to give one an awareness of Christ's presence, the sense of oneness with God (169-170), and implies thereby that Seymour's sainthood was based on an understanding of that oneness, not on a complete achievement of it.

Zooey's clarification of the other point is just as crucial. Franny wishes to have the holy life without the distractions of the crude, unenlightened worldly society. It is a dangerous desire and the one which caused Seymour himself to founder. Seymour (we learn from Buddy in *Raise High the Roofbeam, Carpenters*) had already achieved a kind of detachment which left him unable to communicate with the "normal" world. That, of course, is not good Zen, and Seymour tried to remedy the situation, but in attempting to relocate himself within society, through marriage and psychoanalysis, he cracked up and finally killed himself.[8] Zooey saves Franny from the same potential fate. He discourages Bessie from sending her to a Catholic psychiatrist with the reminder that such treatment had driven Seymour to suicide. In that manner, by making her grasp the necessity of living one's holiness through one's vocation, he helps Franny to forego the conflict between sanctity and worldliness that killed Seymour.

Zooey's help comes at a fortunate moment, for Franny's reaction against normal society, the heritage of her Seymour-Buddy education, had already taken on pathological proportions. She has arrived at the place where her professors and fellow students all appear phony, where her projected acting career seems phony, where life itself is phony, and a fakery. Even though her feeling is exaggerated, it has arisen from a recognition of the shallowness of her fellows, and that is what makes her desperate. Within the existential context, her condition would be described as the sense of meaninglessness.

8. James E. Bryan in "Salinger's Seymour's Suicide," *College English,* XXIV (December, 1962), 226-29, views Seymour's trouble with the world as sexual. The article is ingenious, but I am not quite convinced.

It is prompted not only by her acute religious sensitivity but especially by the superficial values of the culture in which she moves. Zooey, in his bathroom satire, epitomizes the contempt the Glasses share for the comfortable and popular Protestantism that is blind to deep-seated spiritual needs. His sarcastic advertisement for a little inspirational book is a barely disguised reference to Norman Vincent Peale and the magic-formula Christianity he represents (114-15). It is that sort of phoniness that bothers Franny most, for she sees behind the façade of religiosity and is distressed to find nothing there. The apparent universality of meaninglessness drives her quite literally to despair. Zooey accuses Franny of deliberately having her nervous breakdown at home (159, 194), and although he is somewhat unjust (her initial collapse was while on her date in New Haven), he indicates a certain truth: Franny comes home because it is the only place for her where there is no fakery. There, as Zooey assures her, she will find honesty if not solace (194). And it is, naturally, at home that she finds her cure, for the answer to phoniness is verity, and it is only in the atmosphere of truthfulness that she can find meaning.

Franny's cure, which is simultaneously the positive resolution of her religious crisis, involves a bigger dose of the truth than she had bargained for. The problem of phoniness has its seat in the individual ego, and the ego is as much Franny's trouble as it is the trouble of the phonies.[9] The difference is that in Franny it manifests itself in what Zooey calls piousness, itself a form of hypocrisy, unconscious though it may be. To be sure, Franny is aware of her own self-centeredness; she cries out against the torture of her ego (29).

Her complaint echoes the existentialist disgust with the ego, and Salinger in fact plants the names of writers here and there who dealt extensively with that disgust. Kafka and Rilke are mentioned, existential expositors of the egotistical dilemma both, as is Kierkegaard's *Fear and Trembling,* certainly one of the original works treating the problem of the individual and his being. Franny's egocentricity takes a subtle turn. Her awareness of it leads her to abandon a promising acting career, obviously the ideal vocation for indulging the ego, and to turn instead toward a private saintliness. Yet her attitude has not really changed. Instead of becoming a good

9. According to Mary McCarthy in "J. D. Salinger's Closed Circuit," *Harper's Magazine* (October, 1962), pp. 46-48, it is Salinger's trouble as well.

actress, she is determined to be a successful saint, and that by way of her gimmick: repeating the Jesus Prayer until she forces a vision of God. Franny misses the point of the prayer. The incessant iteration of the petition—a plea to Christ for mercy—is supposed to lead one first into humble contemplation of Christ and thereby into an unbroken consciousness of his presence, the classic goal of all Christian mysticism. Franny, in her self-centeredness, sees the prayer only as a means to a selfish end: making God show himself and thereby prove to her that he exists (39).

Franny's cure is a painful one, for in effecting it, Zooey makes her see her selfishness. The positive aspect of his scolding is in showing her the transforming element that she lacks: a right understanding of love. Salinger, alias Buddy, informs the reader at the beginning of Zooey that what follows is not religious or a mystical tale but a complex love story (49). That is more than Salinger's double talk. Franny's cure involves three steps concerned with love. First the explanation of what love is not. Second is the realization that Franny is already surrounded by love through her family. Third is the revelation that genuine love means the love of mankind.[10]

Zooey first exposes Franny's false concept of love—the saintly, sentimental kind—by referring her to an adolescent experience in which she, age ten, loudly rejected Jesus for his rude manner of cleansing the temple and turned to Buddhism (162 ff.). Franny has mistaken lovableness for love, and in her tenderheartedness has been shocked at the New Testament Jesus who employed love as a powerful, transforming force. Franny's repudiation of that kind of love is necessarily related to her self-love; it is again the ego at work, for she has not really wanted a love to change her life. Instead, she has been trying to force the religious experience to take place on her own terms, more as a confirmation of her personal philosophy than as the introduction to a new perspective of life.

Having properly shaken his sister with that analysis, Zooey goes on to argue that she doesn't recognize genuine love in action when she sees it. Since being home she has been catered to and fussed

10. Salinger is also technically correct in disavowing the mysticism of the story. Properly speaking, it is not mystic because true mysticism, at least traditional mysticism, has as its goal the achievement of spiritual union with Christ at the expense of worldly communion. One turns away from human entanglements in order to find God exclusively in nature and in oneself. Franny finds Christ in the world, and although the moment of revelation that leads her to Christ is ecstatic, the foundation for her experience is not.

over by her parents, but she has used theii concern mainly to further nurture her breakdown. For Zooey, the parental love is as religious as real love can be, even though expressed in everyday gestures (194). Having established the locus of love in daily existence and in normal surroundings, Zooey takes the final, and revelatory, step. Talking to Franny on the telephone from Seymour's room (the holy place), he convinces her that her threefold problem of the ego, of phoniness, and of sainthood can be solved by the right understanding and use of love: by serving, and thereby loving, her fellows in the vocation she has chosen. The way to cope with the ego, she learns, is to take its force and sublimate it to its good and natural end.[11] Since her desire is for acting, Zooey encourages her to go at it with religious dedication (197), to develop her talent for all it is worth. To counter phoniness, he advises her to work for professional perfection. Most important, he tells her that she will find the road to sainthood not in communing with lovable people, but in acting before all kinds of individuals, no matter how unlovable they may be. Zooey refers to the statement of Jesus that the Kingdom of God is within one. What Franny has to learn is that it is around one as well.[12]

Franny's experience takes place through a symbolism, both conscious and unconscious on the part of those involved, that provides the necessary emotional dimension. At the core of the symbolism is Seymour. Christ figure or not, Seymour is the one who has gone away so that he might be with his loved ones more fully, and it is by his vision that they live.[13] The saving advice that Zooey gives to Franny is not really his own at all but goes back to Seymour, who had transmitted it to Buddy. Further, it is the ritual aspect of

11. Cf. Alan W. Watts' treatment of the problem of the ego according to Zen doctrine: *The Way of Zen* (New York: Mentor Books, 1959), p. 145. In the spontaneity toward which Zen strives, the individual ego becomes "annihilated in its own trap." The uncontrolled self, expressing itself spontaneously, overcomes the self-consciousness of the ego. Similarly for Franny, in learning to do what her natural desire leads her to do, namely, to act, she supersedes the force of the ego as the self-aware controlling *I*. In Zen terms, she becomes what she is, and not what she thinks she should be.

12. Thus the liberal nineteenth-century translation of Jesus' words as "the Kingdom of God is in your midst" would apply to Franny's situation. Here again is also Zen. The Godness in all aspects of life is a basic assumption of Zen; its realization in one's own life is a part of the *satori* experience. Cf. Suzuki, pp. 125 ff.

13. Bryan, therefore, is right in describing Seymour, however facetiously, as "a sort of Holy Spirit to his siblings." P. 226.

Zooey's telephone call to his sister that helps her as much as the message. Having made the proper preparations (the handkerchief on the head, the meditation, reading the Seymour scripture), Zooey calls from the shrine of Seymour's room, and even when his impersonation of Buddy (the next best to Seymour) fails, the words from the room are the ones that heal Franny. Finally, the reconciling vision of the Fat Lady as Christ is Seymour's. He had transmitted it to both Zooey and Franny; now it becomes Franny's vehicle of re-entry to meaningful existence. It is Seymour's ideal of love, then, transforming the ego, disarming the phonies, exemplified in his own kind of saintliness, that heals Franny. In learning Seymour's ideal she is freed from the ghost of Seymour himself and can pursue her new life in spiritual freedom.

If Salinger's story, for all its ingenuity, does not quite ring true, it is because he finally falls prey to the sentimentalization and superficiality that his characters claim to despise. That double fault focuses upon one point: Salinger's inability or unwillingness to see the existence and power of evil. The Glasses are all saints from the start; their problem is not in achieving goodness but perfection. They do not experience the fundamental maliciousness of human nature, only a malingering nastiness that can be overcome by new attitudes. It is too bad that Salinger's solution at last is little more than a variation of the power of positive thinking. Franny's conversion is just a transference from one kind of illusion to another. Her ego was simply the wrong kind of ego; the phoniness she abhorred is exorcized by another sort, couched in the duplicity of Zooey's telephone call; the love itself that "saves" her is a projection of the Glass narcissism that Seymour and the others have mistaken for a univeral force. Franny's little breakdown gets only the cheap cure it deserves, and no amount of first-rate prose can make the situation as persuasive as those in the other novels. Salinger is certainly free to present his own kind of religion, but the spirits he evokes desert him. The story is not good Christianity and not good Zen and not good existentialism. The result is not an achieved eclecticism but an amalgamation that loses in depth what it gains in breadth. One is, in the end, doubly disappointed in a fictional attempt at depicting the religious crisis that is overwhelmed by its own religiosity.

6. FURTHER CONSIDERATIONS

Having ended on a negative note with Salinger, I hasten to reassert my double intention in the study as a whole: to point out (1) the propensity of certain young contemporary novelists toward the use of the religious crisis as the focal point of their treatment of man and his situation; (2) the approximation by those novelists of modern theological positions in the vocabulary, imagery, and especially in the problematics of their characters' situations.

A number of related questions arise naturally in connection with the demonstration of these propositions. First, one is led to inquire why four talented writers representing a single generation and the unity in diversity of postwar American culture should all, at about the same time, turn to religion as a serious theme for their fiction. Two reasons suggest themselves, the first pointing to the culmination of a certain trend and the second to what is perhaps the beginning of a new one. The first reason is that modern novelists, as products of the society they live and create in, are likely to present in their works the prevailing mood of the time. It is by now a truism that the American spirit has been transformed from the optimism of the early-middle 1800's to the bewildered pessimism of the present. As R. W. B. Lewis puts it in *The American Adam*, "A century ago, the challenge to debate was an expressed belief in achieved human perfection, a return to the primal perfection. Today the challenge comes rather from the expressed belief in achieved hopelessness."[1] It is not surprising, then, that the pessimism has infected the younger novelists as well. Charles I. Glicksberg says:

The writers of today are members of a sick as well as a lost generation; a race of spiritual hypochondriacs, obsessed with thoughts of nothingness, destruction, and death, they teeter nervously on the edge of a nervous breakdown. Modern novelists, engaged in tracing the physiognomy of their culture, find themselves increasingly concerned with themes of abnormality, maladjustment, frustration, sadism, alienation, guilt, cruelty, metaphysical homelessness, loss of faith.[2]

---

1. (Chicago: University of Chicago Press, 1955), pp. 9-10.
2. *Literature and Religion* (Dallas: Southern Methodist University Press, 1960), p. 182.

That diagnosis may be overdramatic, but it is true nonetheless. It applies to the accepted great and good novelists of our time—Fitzgerald, Hemingway, Faulkner, Steinbeck—but particularly to the generation represented in the four writers I discussed. Yet the young writers, I think, have experienced the pessimism with a greater intensity than the novelists before them. The "lostness" of Fitzgerald and the early Hemingway was certainly genuine, but at the same time it was a pose, and with that pose it took on a kind of integrity that made possible the encounter, without cracking up, with a hostile universe. Steinbeck has always been sustained by a nature mysticism, and Faulkner continually reaffirmed his faith in the ability of man to endure.[3]

Styron and confreres, however, as strictly post-war artists, have not had the "lost" stance, nor the refuge of nature, nor an encompassing myth to inspire them. The fashionable nihilism of the twenties has become absolute despair, nature itself has been atomicized, and the American myth from whatever region has lost its efficacy. The young writers have actually reached the "achieved hopelessness"

3. There is always the danger of too stark a black and white contrast. Charles H. Foster, in "The 'Theonomous Analysis' of American Culture" (Studies in American Culture, Joseph J. Kwiat and Mary C. Turpie [eds.] [Minneapolis: University of Minnesota Press, 1960], p. 196) calls attention to the constructive purpose of those major American literary figures: "We have been obliged to recognize that Hemingway, Eliot, Faulkner, and the mature F. Scott Fitzgerald were engaged not in expressing a secular and rationalistic organization of subjective experience but in depicting and criticizing with the most moral concern the spiritual emptiness, the emotional aridity of the human condition in our America." Similarly, Armand Henry Ulbricht in an unpublished dissertation, "The Trend Toward Religion in the Modern American Novel, 1925-1951," shows how writers such as Dreiser, Lewis, Hemingway, Wilder, and Faulkner were forced by the chaos of the time toward a sympathetic consideration of religion, even though he concludes that the religious content of their novels is relatively weak. My private opinion on Faulkner is that he has always been ultimately Christian, Irving Howe's criticism notwithstanding. Faulkner himself has maintained it, e.g., Faulkner in the University, Frederick L. Gwynn and Joseph L. Blotner (eds.) (Charlottesville: University of Virginia Press, 1959), p. 203, for whatever that may be worth, while at least a half-dozen of his novels have employed Christian imagery and even a Christian theology that can be ignored only by losing oneself in the intricacies of the southern myth. As for the other three —Fitzgerald, Hemingway, and Steinbeck—they have lived and created for the most part in a nonteleological world which by the very absence of divine guidance, and thus the absence of responsibility to a divinity, becomes a somewhat more bearable place to live. Despair and nothingness are in themselves teleological concepts and therefore have no real place in the fiction of the naturalists.

that Lewis mentions and have had to do something about it. They have taken two steps: first they have depicted and utilized that hopelessness honestly and then moved *through* it to a new affirmation. The depiction of the negative is not hard to detect. In two of the novels examined, for example, Styron and Updike have gone the limit in presenting depravity and perversion as a metaphor of life lived without spiritual orientation. A test may be that the sexuality of their characters invites no quickening response but profound aversion. Similarly, Roth, without so graphically probing the limits of despair, has managed to imply the demonic nature of man and his world by stressing the final helplessness of his fictional figures. It is a difference of technique, not of philosophy.

The point is that it has become impossible for the young novelists to draw inspiration from the idea of a negative universe, as did the naturalists, for the naturalist vision has lost whatever heroic connotations it may have had and become sterile. The new writers, caught in the nihilism that was their legacy, have had to supersede it in order to continue creative writing.[4] They have been forced into the second step, the exploration of the spiritual, as a new source of inspiration. They have thus culminated the naturalist movement, have taken it to its logical conclusion, and initiated a new impulse that necessarily includes affirmation or at least once again the possibility of affirmation. And any sort of spiritual affirmation will have to speak to the religious dimension.[5]

That brings us to the second reason for the present interest in religion. In seeking to articulate the new affirmation, the young writers have had the help of the only Western philosophy that has faced nihilism squarely and provided an answer to it: I refer, of course, to existentialism, which like the writers themselves has grown out of nihilism, and which has revived the spiritual aspect of life as significant in its own right. Herbert W. Schneider explains the role of existentialism thus:

What has happened since the days of William James is that the religious phenomena which were then examined as vagaries of consciousness, have become objective material for existential analysis.

4. Cf. Jack Ludwig, *Recent American Novelists*, University of Minnesota Pamphlets on American Writers (Minneapolis: University of Minnesota Press, 1962), p. 7, for examples.
5. Having absorbed Leslie Fiedler's anathema against vestiges of positive perspectives in the novel (pp. 4 ff.), one is fearful of even mentioning the

46

Existentialism represents the de-psychologizing of mystic and sinful states. . . . What to James was a conversion of religious appetites is now a cultural transformation.[6]

In my analysis of the four novels, the pervasive influence of existentialism, particularly in its Christian direction, has been apparent. Of the theologians I employed for interpretive backgrounds, Tillich and Buber are primary contributors to existential thought; Niebuhr's theology had existential origin; and even the Zen Buddhism to which Salinger is attracted has remarkable affinities (noted by Suzuki himself) with existentialism.

It is largely because of existentialism that these writers have been able to make the religious experience central and plausible. It has allowed each author to treat the spiritual crisis earnestly. Each considers it a valid phenomenon of human life and has enough faith in its impact upon the individual to use it as the structural framework or climax (or both) of his book. The climax of *Set This House on Fire* is Cass Kinsolving's confrontation with nothingness, his contemplation of family murder and suicide, and his acceptance of being. *Rabbit, Run* is constructed around the continuing crisis of Harry Angstrom; *Letting Go* builds up through some six hundred pages to the spiritual disintegration of Gabe Wallach; *Franny and Zooey* is developed around Franny's nervous breakdown and has its high point in the moment of her recovery. Since the religious crisis in each novel is not explained psychologically or sociologically but in its own terms, it receives its own kind of integrity that affects the novel as a whole. In answer to the question, then, of why the four novelists have turned to religion, one must reply that the sterility of nihilism has impelled them, while the promise of existential analysis has invited them, to it.

A second question involves the farther-reaching implications of the new interest in religion. To what extent do the four novelists really stand for the new generation, and what chance is there of

---

affirmation that the religious experience involves. Yet I take comfort in the fact that of the four novels analyzed here, the weight of three is upon Fiedler's "negative," with precisely the force of the negative bringing about the "conversion" or judgment. And even in *Franny and Zooey*, the one work guilty of a generally positive approach, the sarcasm and irony help offset a possible unwelcome piousness.

6. *Religion in 20th Century America* (Cambridge: Harvard University Press, 1952), p. 190.

the religious impulse subjecting itself to orthodoxy? Regarding the first part of the inquiry, there is sufficient evidence that the four are representative rather than exclusive. One could, for example, conduct the same sort of study with Bernard Malamud, Saul Bellow, and Flannery O'Connor, and to a somewhat lesser extent, with James Baldwin and Carson McCullers. Moreover, I think that if anything I have been too cautious rather than too free in attributing theological sophistication to the postwar generation. In an age when Nietzsche and Kierkegaard and Unamuno, even Buber and Tillich, have become required reading for anyone with the intellectual awareness that the young writers have exhibited, it would be foolish to continue reading and discussing them as if they were still subsisting on the positivist diet of the twenties and thirties.[7] I do not believe that the correspondences presented in this study are merely coincidence but rather that the current philosophical and theological discussion (which on the Continent really goes back to the second and third decades of this century and is finally catching on among us now in America) has already had greater cultural resonance than we have realized. Back in 1949 Horace Gregory ventured the cautious statement that "among younger writers we can discern a subcurrent of religious belief, that is very, very strong, yet only a few novelists of our time have had the art to treat the subject of religion seriously."[8] And in 1952 Amos Wilder reported, "Large strata and movements in the western world are outside the church. But the religious tradition operates in them still in an indirect and disguised way. The river has gone underground; it has not ceased to flow."[9]

7. Nor, on the other hand, do I want to pretend that a fine novelist such as Robert Penn Warren does not exist, nor that the religious novel has ever lost its popularity in America. The point is that a writer like Penn Warren, with his humanist-Christian orientation, is a notable exception among American writers, while almost any critic would assert, *ipse dixit*, that the religious novels of Lloyd Douglas, Frank Slaughter, or Taylor Caldwell are simply not good literature.

8. "Mutations of Belief in the Contemporary Novel," in *Spiritual Problems in Contemporary Literature*, Stanley Romaine Hopper (ed.) (New York: Torchbook, Harper & Row, 1957), p. 44. Quoted by permission of the publisher.

9. *Modern Poetry and the Christian Tradition* (New York: Charles Scribner's Sons, 1952), xii. Quoted by permission of the publisher. At seeming odds with that opinion are such statements as the one by Glicksberg (p. 188) that "though there are some signs of a spiritual revival in contemporary letters, the religious consciousness, at least in its traditional form, seems to have largely disappeared." But the contradiction is only on the surface. Both writers make essentially the same point: it is the traditional religious form

What we are witnessing now, I suggest, is the emergence of the religious awareness among the novelists from the underground, the growth of the "subcurrent" into a considerably stronger flow.

Concerning the second part of the question, it does not appear likely that the new religious interest will solidify into dogma. Although the novels I discussed are theologically oriented, they are never doctrinaire. Unlike Graham Greene or François Mauriac, the four authors are not merely absorbed in giving flesh and blood to metaphysics;[10] unlike the second-rate religious fictioneers, and in spite of an emphasis upon the necessary crisis aspect of the religious experience, they do not sacrifice plausibility in order to bring about the miraculous conversion at all costs; they do not set an elaborate stage to enter *fides qua machina*. For them it is not a matter of creating figures to fit a given solution but of presenting individuals in dilemmas that are first characteristically human and then open to theological definition. Both a literary and a theological fairness are involved, in that none of the protagonists is a type nor are the solutions typed. Examples yes; types never. In the employment of theological insight without surrender to theologizing, in the maintenance of novelistic standards without distorting the religious sensitivity, lies much of the power of the four works and the potential of a future fiction that will treat seriously the religious motif.

The final and perhaps most crucial question is, what effect should the new religious impulse in American fiction have upon theological and literary criticism? For the theologian, it should mean the beginning of a new attitude, whereby he will have to accept the literary imagination not only as a fruitful source of illustration for the validity of his own propositions but as a significant formative force in the definition of his tenets. He should no longer be able to point to the barrenness of the contemporary novel as proof of man's need

---

that has vanished from the arts, not the underlying religious consciousness. It is that consciousness which has "gone underground," and which, I maintain, is now emerging in a new form.

10. Sean O'Faolain, in *The Vanishing Hero* (Boston and Toronto: Atlantic-Little, Brown, 1956), has criticized the Catholic novelists thus: "It has well been said that Greene, Mauriac and Bernanos return us to the medieval world, as if the great humanist tradition had never happened" (pp. 45-46), and: "Greene is not primarily interested in human beings, human problems, life in general as it is generally lived; . . . what he is writing is not so much novels as modern miracle plays" (p. 65). Quoted by permission of the publisher.

of the gospel, for example. Instead, he should be ready to honor the reality of the imaginative perspective even as it invades his own discipline and deals with the religious experience in fictional terms. The interplay has been going on among the truly great theologians and truly great novelists for years. Barth and Berdyaev were inspired and motivated by Dostoevski; Tillich has learned from Kafka. Philosophers such as Kierkegaard and Buber have united the imaginative and discursive approach with singular success in their writings. Now, with the rehabilitation of religion in American fiction a likelihood, the theologian should be prepared to read the young writers not just for homiletic ammunition, but also for an occasional answer to spiritual problems that he can translate into his own terms.

For the literary critic the question is a bit more difficult, since he is still generally quite sensitive to the potential invasion of his territory from other disciplines. That apprehension should not lead him to or hold him in a false isolation. Leslie Fiedler issued the warning over a decade ago that "the 'pure' literary critic, who pretends, in the cant phrase, to stay 'inside' a work all of whose metaphors and meanings are pressing outward, is only half-aware."[11] If that was true then, it is impossible to ignore now. The new situation does not mean necessarily that the critic who will not accept the insights of faith, existential or otherwise, *for himself* will be professionally embarrassed when faced with religion in the novel. It has been possible to interpret *Beowulf* quite well without subscribing to the Germanic-heroic world view. What it does mean is that the critic who approaches the new fiction *parti pris* as though the religious crisis did not exist as a possible component of experience is bound to do injustice to the work. Whether or not he likes it, the teleological dimension has returned to American fiction in the form of the individual religious experience, so that the critic must approach the novel embodying that dimension with a degree of seriousness and objectivity.

It is a curious fact that all four novels examined here received considerably less critical praise than the first novels of each author dealing less directly with the religious experience. Without arguing that any of them has the stamp of great literature upon it (I have stayed away from value judgments, except in the instance of Salinger, where the theological rather than the literary inadequacies

11. Leslie A. Fiedler, "Toward an Amateur Criticism," *The Kenyon Review*, XXI (Autumn, 1950), 564.

FURTHER CONSIDERATIONS

made it necessary), I note that much of the displeasure has been
with the religious concern, as the charges of "hopped-up metaphysics," "too serious," and "non-novel" indicate.[12] Nathan Scott,
who is perhaps far ahead of most of us, expresses the need for the
new attitude with this observation:

The literary work is a trap, but it is a trap that is *oriented* toward
the world of existence that transcends the work—and the work is
oriented by the *vision*, by the *belief*, by the *ultimate concern* of
which it is an incarnation: its orientation, that is to say, is essentially religious. And this is why criticism itself must, in the end, be
theological.[13]

Scott, Amos Wilder, Stanley R. Hopper, and Murray Krieger,
among others, have already pioneered in the application of theological considerations to creative literature. If the intensifying of the
religious element in American fiction, as exemplified in our four
novels, can stimulate a corresponding sharpened focus of theologically aware criticism, the post-Christian era may yet find further
cause to reconsider its heritage.

12. A case in point is the opinion of Robert Gorham Davis in "Styron
and the Students," *Critique*, III (Summer, 1960), 44, that *Set This House
on Fire* should have logically ended with the suicide of Cass Kinsolving. One
can arrive at that conclusion only by denying any validity to Cass' religious
crisis, and the standard of believability here, I think, has been the American
naturalist tradition rather than the one Styron strives to develop throughout
the novel. More cruel is Norman Mailer, who in a recent *Esquire* article,
"Norman Mailer Versus Nine Writers" (July, 1963), pp. 64-69, 105, rec-
ognizes the religious interest in the four novels I discussed (plus others by
Jones, Baldwin, Bellow, Heller, and Burroughs) and even labels it a possible
frontier for contemporary writers, but he considers its treatment by Styron,
Updike, Roth, and Salinger a failure. He calls Styron's book a "bad maggoty
novel" and dismisses the concluding monologue on being and nothingness as
vapid and meaningless. That again, I believe, is an example of a critic's unwillingness to take the theological perspective seriously.
13. P. 38.

51

BIBLIOGRAPHICAL NOTE

The four novels which form the basis of this study are by no means isolated examples of the renewed interest in religion by contemporary American authors. Some other recent novels and short stories illustrating a similar concern with religion are as follows.

First, from the fiction of the four authors discussed here, one should mention Styron's first novel, *Lie Down in Darkness* (Indianapolis: Bobbs-Merrill Co., 1951); Updike's *The Poorhouse Fair* (New York: Alfred A. Knopf, 1959), and *Pigeon Feathers and Other Stories* (New York: Alfred A. Knopf, 1962); Roth's *Goodbye, Columbus*, cited in the notes, comprised of the novelette and short stories; and Salinger's *The Catcher in the Rye* (Boston: Little, Brown & Co., 1951), "Teddy," from *Nine Stories* (Boston: Little, Brown & Co. 1953), and *Raise High the Roofbeam, Carpenters*, and *Seymour —An Introduction*, already cited. A sampling from other writers should include Flannery O'Connor, *Wise Blood* (New York: Harcourt, Brace & Co., 1952); James Baldwin, *Go Tell It on the Mountain* (New York: Alfred A. Knopf, 1953); Saul Bellow, *Seize the Day* (New York: The Viking Press, 1956), and *Henderson the Rain King* (New York: The Viking Press, 1959); Bernard Malamud, *The Assistant* (New York: Farrar, Straus and Cudahy, 1957); Herbert Gold, *Salt* (New York: The Dial Press, 1963); and from Herbert Gold's anthology of short stories, *Fiction of the Fifties* (New York: Doubleday & Co., 1959), George P. Elliott's "Among the Dangs," and J. F. Powers, "The Devil Was the Joker."

Of the four writers studied, only Salinger has received book-length critical treatment. Two of these are collections of essays: Henry A. Grunwald (ed.), *Salinger: A Critical and Personal Portrait* (New York: Harper & Row, 1962); and Malcolm M. Marsden (ed.), *If You Really Want to Know: A Catcher Casebook* (Chicago: Scott, Foresman & Co., 1963). Warren G. French, *Salinger* (New York: Twayne, 1963), presents a comprehensive analysis of Salinger's fiction to date. For the other three, one must depend on articles in the professional journals. In addition to those already cited in the notes, there is the collection of essays edited by Nona Balakian and Charles Simmons, *The Creative Present: Notes on Contemporary American Fiction* (New York: Doubleday & Co., 1963), which presents a more thorough treatment of the same era covered by the Ludwig pamphlet mentioned in chapter 6.

Proof of the intensity of the current dialogue between religion and literature is evident in the large number of interdisciplinary studies. Two written since 1950 from the standpoint of the professional theologian, apart from those already mentioned, are Nathan A. Scott, Jr., *Rehearsals of Discomposure: Alienation and Reconciliation in Modern Literature* (New York: King's Crown Press of Columbia University Press, 1952); and Amos N. Wilder, *Theology and Modern Literature* (Cambridge: Harvard University Press, 1958). Some written since 1950 from the standpoint of the literary critic are Randall Stewart, *American Literature and Christian Doctrine* (Baton Rouge: Louisiana State University Press, 1958); R. W. B. Lewis, *The*

52

Picaresque Saint (Philadelphia and New York: J. B. Lippincott Co., 1959); Murray Krieger, *The Tragic Vision* (New York: Holt, Rinehart & Winston, 1960); Roland Mushat Frye, *Perspective on Man* (Philadelphia: The Westminster Press, 1961); Edwin M. Moseley, *Pseudonyms of Christ in the Modern Novel* (Pittsburgh: University of Pittsburgh Press, 1962); Cleanth Brooks, *The Hidden God* (New Haven: Yale University Press, 1963); and John Killinger, *The Failure of Theology in Modern Literature* (New York and Nashville: Abingdon Press, 1963). Two collections of essays dealing with the interrelationship of religion and literature are Stanley Romaine Hopper (ed.), *Spiritual Problems in Contemporary Literature* (New York: Harper & Brothers, 1952); and Nathan A. Scott, Jr. (ed.), *The Tragic Vision and the Christian Faith* (New York: Association Press, 1957). Two fine introductions to anthologies also treat the subject: John Heath-Stubbs and David Wright (eds.), *Faber Book of Twentieth-Century Verse* (London: Faber and Faber, 1953); and Herbert Gold's already cited *Fiction of the Fifties*. The view of the devil's advocate appears in Fiedler's *No! in Thunder*.

Among the books that examine the general nature of American culture in its relationship to religion, the four-volume *Religion in American Life*, James Ward Smith and A. Leland Jamison (eds.) (Princeton: Princeton University Press, 1961), is the most indispensable tool, particularly Volume II on *Religious Perspectives in American Culture*. Analyses of American Protestantism in its cultural setting are found in H. Richard Niebuhr, *The Kingdom of God in America* (New York: Harper & Brothers, 1937); and Winthrop S. Hudson, *American Protestantism* (Chicago: University of Chicago Press, 1961). A. Roy Eckardt, *The Surge of Piety in America* (New York: Association Press, 1958), appraises postwar Protestant religiosity in this country. Studies giving theological interpretation of the Protestant phenomenon with emphasis upon America are H. Richard Niebuhr, *Christ and Culture* (New York: Harper & Brothers, 1951); and Paul Tillich, *The Protestant Era* (Chicago: University of Chicago Press, 1948), and *Theology of Culture* (New York: Oxford University Press, 1959).

Other books helpful in establishing a fundamental orientation for this study were H. Emil Brunner, *The Theology of Crisis* (New York: Charles Scribner & Sons, 1929); and Marjorie Grene, *Introduction to Existentialism* (Chicago: University of Chicago Press, 1959), which still seems to be the best short treatment of that philosophy.

58829